'A compassionate and fascinating insi where he is today, how he got here a future. Terry Colling acknowledges heartfelt sense of alienation from the peers and, most importantly, from th seek more love, intimacy and self-wo choices in life, for women who strive to bridge the gap sexes and for all professionals working in the field of personal growth and relationships.'

Dr Rosie McInnes

'Thank heavens for Terry Colling. Most women long to understand men but have confused expectations, as do many men. *Beyond Mateship* throws light on a communications problem that must be eradicated if men and women are to live in harmony. It is essential reading.'

Ita Buttrose

'For far too long, Australian men have been hiding behind the socio-sexual barrier of so-called mateship. Quite appropriately, Terry Colling calls this hoary old ultra-Ocker notion and hang-up into serious question. Surely there has to be something after mateship for Australian men? This self-effacing book could take us out of that gender-bind (ironically, very comfortable and womb-like) into a brave new world of men, women and children! We may even enjoy ourselves out there — let alone learn something of a fuller life. ''Blokedom'' can be painfully predictable. For starters, it's chockers with blokes . . . !'

George Negus

'Terry Colling, a marriage guidance counsellor well-known for his insight and expertise, has written a timely book which speaks to the struggles of Australian men coming to terms with the changes occurring in their private lives. Both men and women will benefit greatly from the knowledge and understanding he demonstrates of the male psyche.'

Bettina Arndt

'It's good to see a book written from a man's perspective, and to get a better idea of how men tick. Communication is the keynote to relationships, business and sport — this book gives an insight into how to bridge the communications gaps that sometimes appear, especially between men and women.'

Simon O'Donnell

DEDICATION

This book is dedicated to all the men who are prepared to meet the challenge of the twenty-first century, and who can be

— strong without hardness
— soft without fear
— powerful without oppression
— gentle without shame
— knowledgeable without arrogance
— nurturing
— led with humility
— themselves with joy.

BEYOND MATESHIP
Understanding Australian Men

TERRY COLLING

SIMON & SCHUSTER
AUSTRALIA

BEYOND MATESHIP: Understanding Australian Men

First published in Australasia in 1992 by
Simon & Schuster Australia
20 Barcoo Street, East Roseville NSW 2069

A Paramount Communications Company
Sydney New York London Toronto Tokyo Singapore

National Library of Australia
Cataloguing in Publication data

Colling, Terry, 1932-
Beyond mateship : understanding Australian men.

Bibliography.
Includes index.
ISBN 0 7318 0264 0.

1. Men – Australia – Psychology. 2. Interpersonal relations.
3. Sex role – Australia. I. Title.

305.320994

Designed by Kathie Baxter Smith/Design Smiths
Index by Jill Matthews
Typeset in Australia by Accuset Phototypesetting P/L
Printed in Australia by The Book Printer

Cover photograph: The Boys on the Beach (Bondi, 10 October 1932). From the Late S.J. Hood Collection, State Library of New South Wales.

CONTENTS

ACKNOWLEDGMENTS

As always, my deepest thanks to my wife, Pam, who has put up with me, argued with me, supported me, made tea and sandwiches, rubbed my back, typed the manuscript from my longhand scrawl, sworn at the computer and threatened to kill me if I ever wrote another book.

My gratitude also to my son Paul, who answered our calls when the wretched computer refused to do what we asked of it and who, motherlike, humoured us into learning how to make friends with the monster instead of smashing it.

I must thank the rest of my family for their enthusiasm support and willingness to restrain their groans when the subject of 'the bloody book' was raised.

My thanks to the men in the groups which I conducted to help me write this book. Through their honesty, openness, pain and humour, they showed me and each other that beneath the male façade there is a rich seam of emotional gold crying out to be tapped. The countless hours of working together reassured me that the intimacy we all seek is well within reach. I'm indebted to them all, and have included their comments, anonymously, throughout this book.

I am grateful to Kirsty Melville, my publisher, who showed from the start her belief in the book, and also to Jacqueline Kent, my editor. Jacquie edited my first book, was unavailable for the second and, thank God, helped with the third. She is a great editor and a good friend, who makes me laugh and believe in myself. When I read her comments on the edited pages, it was as if she was in the room talking to me. Thanks also to Narelle Segecic who was given the difficult task of bringing it all together.

My thanks to Dr Don Edgar and the staff at the Institute of Family Studies in Melbourne for the use of their excellent research facilities. And to Peter Fenton, for permission to quote from his poem that heads the section on men and sport in Men Together, page 134.

It is impossible to do more than say a general 'thank you' to the countless clients and friends who have — unwittingly — contributed to this book. This is their book.

Mateship. A code of conduct among men stressing equality and friendship etc (*The Macquarie Dictionary*).

Mate. Companion, fellow worker, form of address among equals, especially sailors or labourers. 2. one of a pair, especially of birds; fitting partner in marriage etc (*Concise Oxford Dictionary*).

'When I told the women in the office that I was in a group of men gathering material for a book on men, they said, "We'll tell you all about men". That's the standard reply.'

'There's a deep longing in me for friendship that allows me to share my deepest thoughts, longings, feelings. There's usually no depth to conversations, the bravado always gets in the way, it's all so inauthentic.'

INTRODUCTION

In the last twenty-five years or so, most of the books examining the relationship between men and women have been written by women. Coming from a feminist perspective, they have addressed the ways women have, both collectively and individually, been exploited by men. A handful of popularist books by men have attempted to address the issue of an appropriate male response to the women's movement. But most of these seem to point men in a regressive direction, calling upon them to reconnect with archetypal male images that have little relevance to modern society or to issues of equality.

The difference between women's perception of men and men's perception of themselves is so great that the lack of books about how men see themselves is exceedingly puzzling. The lack of written material on men as people, as opposed to men as heroes or villains, is surprising. Walk into any good bookshop and ask for the section on women, and you will be shown shelf after shelf on women's issues. But ask the same question about books on men, and the assistant will probably look at you blankly and perhaps point out the section on men's health. The last time I attempted this exercise in Sydney's largest and best known bookshop, I was eventually shown three or four books, with the helpful assistant explaining that 'there wasn't much call for books about men'.

This is true outside Australia as well. In *The Family Therapy Networker*, a U.S.-based newsletter, R. S. Pasick wrote of his search for similar material about men:

> My first research assault was on Borders, a famous bookstore in Ann Arbor, Michigan, where I vaguely remembered

> having seen some books in a back corner. What grabbed me when I walked in this time, however, was the women's studies section, a vast wall of floor-to-ceiling shelves crammed with titles about the history, habits, religions, ideas, politics and sex lives of women. Included was a healthy clutch of books by women about men, with such titles as *Men Are Just Desserts*, *Men Who Hate Women and the Women Who Love Them* and *Secrets About Men Every Woman Should Know* (I wanted to read that one myself).
>
> I asked an employee where the men's section was and was shown to the men's room . . . he pointed to a section in the middle of the store. Sure enough, there was a row of books labelled 'Men' right under a more prominent sign saying 'Homosexuality'.

Given these examples, it is hardly surprising that both men and women are ignorant about men's self-concept. It seems to be the best-kept secret of the century. In addition, there is a gulf in perception between women and men about who a man is and this needs to be urgently addressed; it is central to the relationship between them. Without a shared reality, and operating from different frames of reference, how can they hope to find a common purpose? Trying to build a marriage and a family when the man and the woman are working to different blueprints and speaking different languages becomes a very difficult task — particularly when both partners are mostly unaware of what those differences are and act as if they were working from the same data.

As men represent approximately half of the world's population, the way they see and feel about themselves will have a great bearing on the kinds of societies we create. One thing is clear — unless we are willing to ask questions of men and listen to the answers, we will be inflicting on them the same crime of which women accuse them: 'You don't listen.'

Beyond Mateship looks at Australian men today, and

examines how they are experiencing life in relation to the major facets of their roles: as men, with other men, with the women in their lives, their families, their work, their leisure, their sexuality and power.

This book examines the historical conditioning of Australian men which has left them both defensive and defenceless. The outside world, built upon the struggles of an earlier era and represented by the institutions they have created, may be telling them to stay the same but women, and new-found internal voices, are telling them to be different. Men have discovered a new kind of pain — loneliness and longing. For the first time, they are starting to hear from the boys inside themselves who were imprisoned in suits of armour centuries ago and told to be men. They can no longer block out the need for intimacy, friendship, tenderness and creativity; those things dealing with 'being' rather than 'doing'. Having allowed the inner need to reach the surface, it is demanding to be heard.

The challenge for men is to find an identity, a role that will allow them to integrate both parts of their natures — the vulnerable, sensitive boy and the active, pragmatic man. Australian men today, see themselves as urgently needing to address the conflicts between the social expectations of masculinity and their own need for personal and emotional fulfilment.

I believe that, because Australia's early history was harsh and difficult, the first European men who came here had to adapt to their new lives and environment in very specific ways. This involved the development of certain definitely 'Australian' styles of behaviour, usually described by the term 'mateship'. The first part of this book outlines some of the main strands in Australian history that led to these adaptations, and their consequent effects on how Australian men now see themselves and are seen by women.

Part Two deals with the greatest upheaval in the

relationship between men and women — the feminist revolution of the 1960s and 1970s. In a sense this section forms the rest of the book, which deals with the way in which Australian men now see themselves as a result of the feminist movement.

Part Three deals with the problems of male identity and finding suitable role models (fathers, heroes, or something else?) and the fourth part of the book examines key aspects of men's self-perception and roles: sexuality, family issues, work, men together, and the nature of male power, good and bad.

My two previous books, *Relationships* and *Teenagers*, became windows into myself, the first into my role of husband, the second into my role of father. *Beyond Mateship* is a window into myself as a man, and also a look into countless other men who have been my clients. It results from a collective effort that originated in the mid 1960s, beginning in encounter groups with me as a participant, continuing in my training as a marriage guidance counsellor, and contains my shared journeys through joy and pain with innumerable men and women whom I have counselled as individuals, couples, in families and in groups.

To write this book, I conducted a series of men's groups, and recorded and transcribed comments in which the feelings, views, attitudes, hopes and fears of men were laid bare. The men in these groups ranged in age from twenty-seven to fifty-eight and they were single, married, divorced and remarried. They included manual workers, professionals, junior and senior management, self-employed and public servants. They and their partners came from very mixed backgrounds: Aboriginal, Maori, French, German, Dutch, Irish, Scottish, Danish, Italian, Greek, Scandinavian, West Indian, Chinese and British as well as Australian.

It was never intended that the men in these groups should be statistically representative of the Australian male population; just that they should be able to express their attitudes and feelings about being male. What started out as an attempt to establish a basis for verifying those views I had gained about men in contemporary Australian society turned into something much more. I shouldn't have been surprised by the response of the group members, but I was. Almost immediately the men were talking to each other about the most intimate aspects of their lives, things they had never told another living soul.

Needless to say when the original purpose of the groups had been served, the men wanted them to continue, with a different focus, this time to meet their own needs for self-awareness and friendship.

I found these groups immeasurably rewarding, as they revealed a depth of emotion that men rarely expose. Gone was the competitive macho game-playing that we men are so accustomed to encounter in each other's company. It was replaced by a strong sense of purpose to say what we are really like underneath, and to talk of the desperate hunger for friendship and intimacy with other men as well as with women.

If men are to realise the potential they have for self-expression, they will need to create an environment in which new behaviour can have some hope of germinating. This is a major challenge; the risk of losing their identity in developing a new mateship that is different, yet equally closed to women, is great. But in order to be at peace with each other, we need to be at peace with ourselves. It is time for men to come to terms with the various parts of themselves if they are ever to relate effectively and intimately to the women and men of the world.

I hope *Beyond Mateship* will be a small step in this process.

Terry Colling, Sydney 1992

PART ONE
THE DEVELOPMENT OF MATESHIP

. . . in some ways, you know, good comradeship takes the place of friendship. It is different: it has its own loyalties and affections; and I am not so sure that it does not rise on occasion to an intensity of feeling which friendship never touches.

Frederic Manning, *The Middle Parts of Fortune*

THE CONVICTS

Our fathers toiled for bitter bread
While idlers thrived beside them;
But food to eat and clothes to wear
Their native land denied them.
They left their native land in spite
Of royalties' regalia,
And so they came, or if they stole
Were sent out to Australia.

Henry Lawson, 'Freedom on the Wallaby'

Many factors have combined to mould the Australian male and his view of himself, and to see their origins we need to go back to the early days of settlement. Two hundred years ago, the first Europeans were the outcasts of British society — expendable, disposable human flotsam. Until the 1830s, the colony was predominantly a male prison. The convicts were at the bottom of society's pile, and the governors and military were determined to keep them there, by whatever means they had at their disposal. Australia was a brutal place.

In the early eighteenth century, England was experiencing major social change. The impact of the Industrial Revolution on the lives of the ordinary people was profound. As the nation's production moved from rural and cottage industry to massive urban centres with factories employing up to a thousand workers, employers were able to directly control the standards of living in the work place. The Industrial Revolution saw the end of the family as a social and economic unit who worked collectively and lived in a stable society. The means of subsistence now rested on gaining paid labour, and the most likely employees were the women and children. Men could be shipped elsewhere — unemployment, poverty, a population explosion, a high crime rate and overflowing prisons ensured that they were.

Of course, the early convicts were hardly ideal settlers. They had none of the skills necessary to develop a self-reliant society. Most had been city dwellers. Some existed on their wits by thievery, pimping, gambling and practically everything but regular paid work. Their survival largely depended upon their ability to outwit the law and their collective distrust of authority of any kind. Their capture and transportation could be said to indicate that they were losers, even as criminals. The crimes against property for which about three-quarters were transported in the early days required a very different kind of society than the one of which they now formed a part. There were others who had trades — watchmakers, cabinet makers, tailors, glassmakers, potters, jewellers and so on — who could only flourish where there was an urban population and a middle or upper class. But the new colony needed brickmakers, stonemasons, shipwrights, carpenters, blacksmiths; tradesmen and skilled workers, who perhaps represented about ten per cent of the workforce.

These tradesmen faced a totally alien environment. Those who had to rely on local raw materials had to start from scratch in many cases. Men who worked with timber found that almost all the wood was hard as rock, blunting the axes and saws and almost impossible to work. Those on the land had to learn about the crops and the seasons — nothing could be taken for granted.

What did these early settlers think of themselves? Let's take an imaginary convict, Ted, as an example.

Ted was a farm labourer and part-time thief. When he was born the world around him was orderly. The family lived in the cottage that was a part of his father's right as senior herdsman on a large estate in the English midlands. By the time he had reached manhood all that had changed. The estate had been sold to the mill owners to provide space for the housing of the workforce and factory. Coal mining had developed along with the mills to provide steam for the new mill machinery. There had been a massive influx of people from the surrounding countryside and from Ireland to meet the insatiable demand for labour. Wages were constantly being reduced and the most attractive employees were women and children. Their pay was much lower than that of the men and the mills required deftness and keen eyesight and not strength to handle the thread. In many families it was the women and children who supported the household, and Ted's was no exception.

Ted was a three time loser having been convicted on two previous occasions for larceny, he was sentenced to fourteen years transportation in 1792.

Ted lost not only his family and friends, but also his anchor in life — though he had experienced the changes of the Industrial Revolution, Ted's self-identity was still specific to the farm where he had always lived, and the history and culture of an old nation. Now he had to travel 12,000 miles across an ocean he had only heard about. The voyage out was monotonous and brutalising: he and his fellows were cooped up below decks in rough weather with hardly enough room to move. The food was inedible, the stench of close-packed humanity almost worse. The pecking order was soon established: troopers, favoured prisoners, the best fighters, manipulators, crawlers, then the weak right at the bottom.

All Ted's possessions were stolen in the first two days at sea. He had been befriended by another man who said he came from the next town, and suggested they stick together. Ted later found that his new friend was part of a Liverpool gang transported for burglary. All he got for attempting to recover his belongings was a bashing. When he tried to report the events, he was laughed at and told to steal from someone else. So Ted did what most of the other prisoners did. Deciding he could rely only on himself, because neither the system nor his fellow transportees were any use to him, he withdrew into himself.

When he arrived, things were almost worse. It is difficult to overestimate the effect of the climate and landscape on the mind, emotions and actions of a man like Ted. For one thing, he had left behind a land that was soft and green, that had been settled for thousands of years, where order and predictability were taken for granted, where everybody knew his place. Now Ted was a convict in a land peopled by who he saw as totally alien and unfriendly blacks, where everything was upside down: trees shed bark instead of leaves; torrential downpours replaced light rain; the sun was merciless instead of warming; the animals and plants were unfamiliar and men could be speared, shot or flogged.

Even harder to bear was the loneliness, and the knowledge that he belonged nowhere. He was deprived of the place in life that he had taken for granted, the place carved out for him by generations of men at home. He missed his family desperately and worried about them, while knowing that he would probably never see them again. He was alone, abandoned, robbed of his skills and family, and without friends. He wanted a mate, somebody to rely on, but his experience on the ship had taught him caution, and he had to learn about trust.

Like the other convicts, he knew he had to survive. To do that, he needed to repress and divert his softer emotions, which could make him vulnerable and open to exploitation. And he also had to learn how to keep out of trouble, how to work the system, whom to work for, whom to avoid.

For Ted and hundreds like him, this was what life in the new colony was like. There were very few women, so men had to learn how to survive without them. The presence of women which — in most instances — moderates the behaviour of men, was missing. (When we look at male societies which exist outside of the institutionalised groups, we get a picture of men behaving in ways that would be less predominant in mixed company.) Robert Hughes, in his book *The Fatal Shore*, writes about the prevalence of homosexuality:

> One would naturally suppose that, in a remote colony whose proportion of men to women varied between 4 to 1 in the city and 20 to 1 in the bush, homosexuality would have flourished. So it did, especially on the chain gangs and in the outer penal settlements; but it did not leave much official evidence behind.

But economically things improved by gradual stages, and the convicts who survived grew healthier and more robust than they had been on arrival. The new colony became a viable entity.

But men's view of themselves had changed irrevocably. In the face of an alien, often hostile environment, they developed a frontier survival mentality. And particularly in the early days, men were often united against the authority they despised. The law and its administration were seen by the ordinary man as existing for the primary purpose of keeping him in his place and his superiors on his back. There was little respect for the law, often because those who enforced it were corrupt themselves.

From the earliest days of settlement lawlessness was a part of everyday life, from petty theft and drunkenness to murder and escape (these two were considered equally serious). Anyone who could stick it up the law was seen as 'one of us', particularly as almost all the citizens had at some time or other been victims of the long arm of the law. For many men that arm had held a cat-o'-nine-tails and 500 lashes, little cause for endearment to the system. Is it any wonder that those men who could outwit the law and live in the bush would become free spirits to be admired. The ordinary man and woman had little to fear from the bushrangers as they mostly had nothing worthwhile to steal, so the bushrangers could be seen as latter day Robin Hoods robbing the rich of their undeserved valuables. The reality of their lives didn't have to conform to the myth and romanticism, it was good to get a sense of belonging to the winning side for a change.

The larrikin was therefore also a part of our developing collective identity. His behaviour ranged from the hoodlum to harmless high spirits. Like the bushranger, he had appeal mainly by virtue of his irreverence and cheekiness. The person who is able to flaunt the rules and get away with it, particularly when he doesn't see himself as subscribing to those rules, challenges the timidity of the masses and encourages them to join with him in spirit by identification. By the late 1800s the second and third generation male youths had outgrown their fathers' and grandfathers' fear of authority — they were the currency lads and lasses. With the recklessness of youth, they could afford to cock a snook at society and its keepers. They were emboldened not only by their status as free-born Aussies but by the role models of other free spirits who challenged and won.

Whilst the convicts in New South Wales had to develop a frontier survival mentality to cope with the dual threats of authority and the hostile environment, the convicts in Port Arthur had only the oppressive penal system with which to contend. As a consequence, the mainland fostered a high need for mateship whilst Tasmania became subdued and oppressed by the system. It would seem that the softer landscape and the relative isolation of the population of Tasmania left little room for independent pioneering action, so that progressively the population became as subdued as New South Wales' became unruly.

What made the Australian male experience the frontier in a different way from American or South African pioneers? The difference may be summed up in one word — convict. The Americas were populated by free settlers as well as convicts. The Pilgrim Fathers were idealists, with a strict moral code supported by deep religious convictions. They were a homogenous group who had an abiding belief in themselves. They were joined by other groups who, far from being the outcasts of society, were the epitome of orderliness and social restraint. Similarly, the Dutch Reformers were strict, hard working, family orientated conformists who embodied the same values the early convict settlers had defied.

Another pivotal factor in developing an Australian male identity was the act of stealing land from the Aborigines. The systematic take-over of another's land requires a special kind of rationalisation; the oppressor must repress his natural feelings of pity, self-disgust, fear, compassion and humanity in order to carry out his resolve. He must dehumanise the oppressed and, because our early settlers had been forced to suppress many of their own softer emotions in order to survive, they were able to do this with appalling ease. If the Aborigines retaliated, the whites were driven to rely on each other, and 'mateship' became all the more important. The brutalising effect of the white system left Europeans with very little understanding of the people they oppressed and even less regard for their culture, beliefs and any significance the land might have for them.

As settlement spread westward at the start of the nineteenth century, the cedargetters blazed the trails, cut the timber and paved the way for the farmers who would settle the land and the men who would build the towns. They were necessarily tough and resourceful, and had to live off the land, away from settlements for much of the year. They made money quickly which gave them a heroic aura; they were hard-drinking, hard-living men. And the bush became the place where real men lived.

Like the convicts, the cedargetters, explorers, farmers and other early settlers grew to value reliability, steadfastness, loyalty, ingenuity, courage, toughness and humour. These were the characteristics men needed if they were to survive in Australia. Expression of emotion was frowned upon — it could be a sign of weakness.

And mates were male. Women never became part of this exclusive society. It needs to be remembered that even though the ratio of females to males eventually reached parity, many men's lives were spent mainly in the company of other men. Their occupations as timbergetters, drovers, miners, prospectors, farmhands, shearers or itinerant workers took them away from home and family for months at a time. Women might run farms while their men were away, as well as bring up children, cook and look after the home, but they were still outsiders, not to be trusted or taken entirely seriously. They were different; they couldn't be understood, and they didn't understand blokes either. (The echoes of this exclusivity can be heard today in the TV beer advertisement: 'Mates, mates, they're what this country's made of/They're what your wife's afraid of.')

These, then, became the main elements of the Australian concept of 'mateship', with far-reaching effects on the development and history of the Australian male. This was an unfortunate cornerstone of male identity because, while in the early days it was very functional, it could not evolve into a code of behaviour to suit succeeding generations of men. Mateship flourishes in adversity, without an external threat it often becomes a dysfunctional model.

THE GOLD RUSHES

The night too quickly passes
And we are growing old,
So let us fill our glasses
And toast the Days of Gold;
When finds of wondrous treasure
Set all the South ablaze,
And you and I were faithful mates
All through the roaring days!

Henry Lawson, 'The Roaring Days'

The search for gold which began in the 1850s, attracted a particular kind of migrant: a man (usually a man) who was adventurous, discontented with his lot, and who wanted to make his fortune quickly. These are not usually the characteristics of the law-abiding citizen and, in fact, on the goldfields lawlessness flourished. The gold rushes confirmed the scepticism about authority that had been such a feature of the early days of Australian settlement. The gulf between the ordinary bloke and authority made it all the more imperative to stay with your own kind, to support your mate. Whilst men are essentially socialised to be competitive at an individual level, mateship transcends this so that they will band together for a common purpose in response to an external threat. The competition between individuals on the goldfields would generally be subordinated to the awareness of the collective need.

When people operate at subsistence level, when most of their energies are devoted to scratching a living from the earth, they have very little time for the refinements of polite society. This was certainly true of men during the gold rushes, and it is probably fair to say that the search for gold reinforced those male traits, particularly competitiveness and the distrust of authority, that had been part of the earliest days of convict settlement.

At about the same time as the gold rushes, a whole new group of settlers was emerging: the Irish, fleeing Ireland to seek a new life after the 1847 potato famine. They brought with them a culture of struggle against oppression and poverty that went back hundreds of years. They belonged to the Catholic church which had always represented a major bulwark against the ruling British aristocracy and its ally, the Anglican church.

Those who now saw Australia as their home resented the power structure whereby English legal and judicial institutions directed their lives and taxed their profits. They also felt that the ordinary man's views were less than well represented. The Eureka Stockade incident in 1854 (the miners rebellion on the Ballarat goldfields) brought to a head these feelings of egalitarianism, and formed the push that culminated in Australia being regarded as a crucible for social and political reform by the end of the nineteenth century. The working man now considered himself as good as his master, and as working in a society where there were no bars to achievement except a man's own will and determination.

The process of self-selective migration, combined with the perennial struggles against the land and authority, reinforced the masculinisation of Australian society, bringing forth the role of man the fighter, the 'battler'. It is no coincidence that we have chosen such a word to epitomise the person — often male — who survives against great odds. Its military connotation is unmistakable, speaking of conflict, hardship, and survival. And the concept of the battler was reinforced when, according to popular mythology, Australia 'became a nation', when soldiers fought in the First World War.

AUSTRALIANS AT WAR

> It lay in the mettle of the men themselves. To be the sort of man who would give way when his mates were trusting to his firmness; to be the sort of man who would fail when the line, the whole force, and the allied cause required his endurance; to have made it necessary for another unit to do his own unit's work; to live the rest of his life haunted by the knowledge that he had set his hand to a soldier's task and had lacked the grit to carry it through — that was the prospect which these men could not face. Life was very dear, but life was not worth living unless they could be true to their idea of Australian manhood. Standing upon that alone, when help failed and hope faded, when the end loomed clear in front of them, when the whole world seemed to crumble and the heaven to fall in, they faced its ruin undismayed.
>
> Charles E. W. Bean, *The Official History of Australia in the War of 1914-1918*, vol. 1, *The Story of Anzac*

> Put him in the army, that will make a man of him.

In a way war is made for men because men are made for war. Men are objectified by society in such a way that war can almost seem the climax of their socialisation. As men are required to fight to protect hearth and home, an essential part of their socialisation has to be heroism and the suppression of fear. Along with the fighting of the First World War came rallies, speeches, recruitment parties, music, girls, uniforms — here was a chance to prove your manhood, win the sheilas, get regular pay and have an adventure. Men could see the world at the government's expense, and it was a chance not only to admire heros but to be one.

Women, too, share instincts of aggression. When the First World War broke out, women were at least as enthusiastic for war as men, rewarding the enlistees and ridiculing the others as cowards, not real 'men'. Most of the Australian population saw the First World War as a just war; until the dreadful slaughter at Gallipoli and on the Somme in France in 1916, which forever altered the perception of war as glory.

There exists a great gulf between the popular depiction of war and its reality. I well remember my own experience of the Second World War, when our house was filled with servicemen. I was seven when it started, and thirteen when it ended. I was the youngest male in the family, with four older brothers.

My eldest brother was taken prisoner at Dunkirk at seventeen and spent the rest of his life in a German prison camp. The next was in the Royal Navy for the duration of the war. The third was in the Fleet Air Arm, and the next youngest fought in Malaya. My father was too young for the First World War and too old for the Second, when he did essential war work. My cousin was killed as a glider pilot at the crossing of the Rhine. One brother-in-law was in the RAF, another was in one of the Scottish regiments that went through the desert campaign, one was a Canadian infantryman who landed at Normandy and went to Berlin, and another was killed in Burma with the Chindits.

My father-in-law was a boy soldier who went to the Duke of York Military School in Dover, England, at the age of seven. He went to France as a fighter with the artillery in 1914, and had his fifteenth birthday on the battlefield. In the late 1920s, on the northwest frontier of India, he was stabbed in the arm during a skirmish. He was invalided out at age thirty, without a right arm, to make his way in the world.

What do I know about their experiences? Nothing. They never talked about fear, courage, sacrifice, blood, tears, terror, killing, being shot at, hardship, depravation or starvation. The only memories I was allowed to share were the funny anecdotes: the time my father-in-law got drunk and found himself the next morning minus pay book and trousers; the time my brother, Norman, was bored when on guard duty and was throwing his bayonet at the door to see if it would stick, just when the officer of the watch stepped through; and my brother, Fred, talking about the end of Ramadan being celebrated by the Gurkha soldiers with whom he served. The only information I have is light and dismissive, despite a close and lifelong association with at least eight men whose lives were permanently affected by their experience of war. I admire them for their forbearance, but I'm angry at the code of militarism which, like mateship, makes them prisoners of their own horror.

Australian men had been bred for war. The code of ethics that mateship had given them was perfectly tailored for conflict. Both depended on an external threat; both encouraged the perception of good and evil in black and white terms; both upheld the brotherhood and solidarity which lead to unquestioning loyalty; and both demanded the suppression of tender emotions in order to survive. Rigid conformity, favouring action over words and emotions, and the exclusion of women were perpetuated. It was the army's similarity to contemporary male society that made Australians such effective soldiers. Their larrikinism made them resourceful and unafraid of conflict, and the ordinary soldier generally held the officer class in contempt unless the officers had shown their mettle as men. Anzac Day became Australia's national day, a day for reliving the glory of war and reinforcing the image of a real man, a mate. Men became trapped by their own propaganda.

Whilst the Second World War again produced strong

reinforcement for the concept of mateship, it should be contrasted with the effects of the Vietnam War — where the lack of public support challenged the nature of mateship for the first time. No longer were the protests male dominated. By now, women were playing a significant part in challenging the concepts of male power and domination. Mothers were free to defend their sons' right not to fight for God and country. The power of mateship was being severely eroded.

THE DEPRESSION

> But fathers and sons have problems I think. I sometimes dream about him and struggle to talk to him man-to-man, but I can't. Which reproduces what happened in real life. I think he would have had trouble approving of the erratic, chancy life I've led — the Depression made his generation value the steady job. But he might have adjusted. He died twenty years ago, so I'll never know, which irks me a bit, still.
>
> Peter Corris, in *Yacker 3: Australian Writers Talk About Their Work*, by Candida Baker

Whereas the First World War had massively increased the essential bonding that war brings, the next twenty years were to see a significant reduction in its influence. It is often assumed that hardship, by its very nature, leads to social turmoil and militancy. In fact, it is more likely to lead to lethargy, despair and dissillusionment. The Great Depression of the late 1920s and early 1930s, when upwards of 30 per cent of the working population were unemployed, illustrates this case. The New Guard, which was a secret army formed to combat the perceived threat to national security, need never have existed. Australia was as far from revolution as it ever had been. Whilst the union movement and the emerging Labor and left-wing parties talked about a new world order, most men were doing what people do when they are hungry and homeless — they searched for food and shelter.

The extent to which mateship was influenced by the Depression is hard to judge. On the one hand, large numbers of men took to the bush in search of work —

reinforcing the myth of the resourceful independent swaggie, and building on the belief that the real Australian man was rural rather than urban. On the other hand, male institutions became increasingly less significant as they failed to deliver the basic needs of food, shelter and work which the average man was seeking. The loss of dignity of those men who were no longer able to support their families would have a far-reaching effect on their sense of the need for secure employment for their sons in years to come. The conservatism of these fathers was in part responsible for the rebellion of their children and grandchildren in the 1960s and 1970s.

MEN IN THE UNION

> Australia is internationally renowned as a proud democracy to which one of the world's strongest trade union movements has made crucial contributions. Widely (if hazily) linked in many minds with the strength of our democracy and our unionism is 'mateship'.
>
> Miriam Joyce Dixson, *The Real Matilda*

Unionism played a very significant role in developing and entrenching mateship in Australia. The values of solidarity, struggle, working for the common good against the exploiting bosses fitted the Australian male ethos just as well as war had done. Like the armed forces, the union movement was a male society in which criteria for membership were identical to the codes of mateship developed by the early settlers. Loyalty was more important than life itself, disloyalty was the most heinous crime that existed. In some union towns the stigma of being labelled a 'scab' carried on from one generation to the next.

This sense of belonging to something bigger than themselves, something that gave men a sense of mastery and strength over an oppressive hierarchy, provided a unity of purpose that was very Australian, and became a common bond transcending most other divisions such as language and class. While it was clearly coercive, it was also bonding in the longer term; racism and bigotry were still present, but were overlain with a larger, more common purpose. Like war, unionism produced strange bedfellows. A man could be a 'wog' or a 'reffo', and still be a mate in the union.

This sense of common purpose showed concrete results in the winning of major concessions from employers. It gave men a strong reinforcement of those mateship values they fostered and adopted. In the light of clear evidence that mateship was working to improve men's lives by giving them better pay and conditions and improving the lives of their families, who would question the concept? As the old ad says, 'When you're on a good thing, stick to it'. So mateship, which served the needs of generations, was to demonstrate its continued usefulness.

Who could have predicted a time when it would become as much a liability as an asset? The solidarity that had given men so much was limiting their choices for a different relationship with each other and with women.

THE MENZIES YEARS

> The baby boomer's childhood was the childhood of billycarts, Vicks VapoRub, box-pleated tunics and Smokey Dawson. It was the childhood of cubbies, the Argonauts, musk sticks and 'God Save the Queen'. It was the childhood of the two-parent family and the three bedroom suburban home. It was the childhood with Mum cooking Anzac biscuits for afternoon tea. It no longer exists.
>
> Helen Townsend, *Baby Boomers: Growing up in Australia in the late 1940s, 50s and 60s*

The men who came back from the Second World War participated in a period of unprecedented prosperity that lasted for twenty-five years. The average Australian man could relax: he did not need to experience the type of hardship and masculine exclusivity that had been essential in establishing and maintaining dinkum friendship. The war had been fought, most of the frontiers conquered; men were as good as their masters. They drank at the same clubs, owned their own homes, had boats and caravans. The kids were well fed and better educated than their parents. The only places where the heroic symbols of male identity could still be seen were on the sports fields, in the struggle with the bosses through the union movement, and in the armed forces. Australians were looking for a chance to relax and enjoy the benefits of living in a country that was the envy of most of the world. Prosperity was Australia's for the taking.

The first thing to disturb this sun-drenched paradise was the arrival of television in 1956. Hailed as our coming of age, it gave Australia entry into the wider world, and we became aware of our own insularity for the first time. Television was one of the most revolutionary tools in society; our vulnerability to cultural invasion was never fully realised until it happened. Looking back, it is clear that our comfortable self-satisfaction had to end: the Kennedy assassination, the Vietnam War, the major world events of the 1950s and 1960s intruded into our living rooms and brought to an end our rest.

Migration after the Second World War, however, ensured that the strong national identity that had been developing was not significantly changed — at least, not for a long time. The resettlement of refugees from Europe in the early post-war years was more than outweighed by the voluntary migration of large numbers of people from England, the Mother Country.

The Poms who represented the bulk of the early post-war migrants brought their families with them. They were carefully screened to fit the image Australia held of itself; a land of great promise for young white Anglo-Saxon families. The new migrants had self-confidence and high hopes; they saw themselves as belonging through right of language and common heritage.

When I arrived in Australia from England with my family in 1958, I was twenty-six years old and my wife, Pam, was twenty-two. We had two children, aged three and nine months. By the time we arrived, the Cold War was at its height, the Korean War was stalemated, and the world was becoming familiar with the domino theory of Communist expansion. However, little information on these events filtered down to the individual level of Australian society. Most of us couldn't afford a telly and videos were unheard of. Men's and women's lives were punctuated by mundane things such as paying the bills, buying the food, raising the children, having a house of your own and not getting pregnant. We initially settled in a small company town in Gippsland, a town essentially created to supply labour for the power stations and the open cut mines that fed them.

We lived in a Housing Commission house on a large estate filled with weatherboard houses that were almost identical. We had a dry pan toilet down the yard, a wood stove, a wood copper in the laundry and a chip heater in the bathroom. There were hitching rails outside the pub and some of the stores. The place was closed down tight as a drum by noon on Saturdays, except for the pub and the RSL club.

Then we moved to Melbourne and more familiar urban surroundings. We lived on a new subdivision with dozens of other families, all young and as broke as we were. Most of us lived on one income and struggled to make ends meet, yet there was a great sense of sharing and community. Saturday evening was barbecue night, and we took it in turns to host the street but all the couples brought their own meat and drinks and perhaps a sweet or salad. Big nights out, were trips to the movies in town or dinner at a restaurant. We babysat for each other on these occasions or shared a hired sitter for the special occasions. We all dressed to kill and took photos of each other in our finery. The women sported beehive hairdos and cocktail dresses, and we men wore our suits and ties, left over from the wedding.

When the children were very young, we didn't have TV, and the children tended to play outside until dragged in for a bath and bed. No one ever dreamed they were at risk: we hadn't heard of stranger danger and without mass communication we were blissfully unaware of the big bad world around us. Drugs were things you got from the doctor. Beer and Bex powders were harmless, we bottled our own wine at parties and the environment was under threat, but nobody had told us.

Later on, I remember being fascinated by a documentary on ABC television showing the clearing of the brigalow country by the use of two gargantuan tractors pulling a massive chain between them, and at regular intervals along the chain were what appeared to be steel balls, two or three metres in diameter, the whole contraption simply devastating all in its path. I can still recall the commentary about man's great ingenuity in being able to tame the bush and bring it under cultivation. I felt proud of the achievement; our society was all right, we were all moving in the same general direction. But our children were to inherit a quite different world.

The flow of British migrants like us was overtaken by those from Europe. As most of them were full-fare paying passengers, not ten-pound migrants, few could afford to bring their families with them. So Australia saw a repetition of the influx of single males needing to find a place for themselves in a new land. While these new males had not shared the social history of the Australian male, and consequently were less inclined to share the machocentric bias, they still needed to belong. As Nino Culotta so graphically demonstrated in that classic of the 1950s, *They're a Weird Mob*, to belong you had to adapt to the language and symbols of the dominant culture, or you were relegated to the cultural ghetto.

I shall never forget my initiation into the male cultural obstacle course when I visited an Australian pub for the first time in 1958. It was 5.30 p.m. on a Saturday and, like many others on a hot summer afternoon, I walked off a crowded sweaty train across Flinders Street, Melbourne, and into the pub for a cool, quiet drink.

It is hard to describe the scene and the experience accurately. Men spilled out onto the footpath or sat on the path with their backs to the pub wall. They had rows of glasses lined up beside them while they chatted, smoked and laughed, oblivious of their surroundings. The din was deafening. Bodies filled the room from wall to wall, everybody standing and drinking. Beers were being passed over the heads of the drinkers, who were constantly showered by dripping glasses, orders were being shouted over the top of the general hubbub as people tried to line up enough beers before the bar closed at six.

I was shocked at what seemed like a cattle market atmosphere. Gone was any sense of comfort or any attempt to make the occasion pleasant, here was a place where the sole preoccupation was drinking as fast as possible, because time was at a premium. Amazingly, it was being done with good humour and they really seemed to be enjoying themselves.

I wasn't brave enough or able to shoulder my way to the bar, so I walked down Elizabeth Street for a milkshake.

I was later to be initiated into this male rite of passage by an Australian man who became a great friend. The rules were something like this: you only drank beer (fancy drinks such as gin and tonic, scotch and soda, sherry, port and shandies were for the ladies or the winos); you always stood your shout (bought drinks for all the group); you should never be the last to finish your drink (you'd be holding up the whole school) or you would hear such remarks as, 'It's a very dry argument', or 'I see the tide's out'. Whilst it was possible to refuse another drink, refusal was frowned upon and would be resisted by such comments as, 'Don't you want to drink with me?' or 'Is the Missus counting?' or 'I'll only get you a middy'. Only certain subjects were discussed — work, sport, politics, sex, women (with the exception of wives), fixing the house. Men's talk.

Pubs became social levellers for the migrant male. The Europeans, with their cafes and bar settings in which wine was drunk and games were played, had enjoyed a different style of leisure. In time the migrants established their own social clubs where it was unnecessary for them to try to fit in, they could speak their own language, play their own games and preserve their own culture. The British, of course, had been used to their local pubs that were an integral part of the social life of the community and in which women as well as men congregated for entertainment and relaxation.

THE HIJACKING OF THE AUSTRALIAN MALE

> We used to fight, my dad and I. He'd been through the Middle East in the war, and was your regular digger — he'd march and everything. When the lottery to Vietnam started, I was nineteen and a peace activist. It took us ten years to even speak to each other again.

In the 1960s, with the anti-war movement and the emergence of hippies, the Beatles, and the music and drug scene, the Australian male self-image came under threat for the first time since television. Your average Aussie bloke had to contend with the anti-authority, equality and solidarity bandwagon being driven by long-haired male weirdos with flowers in their hair, wearing what looked like drag.

Furthermore, they had a new, almost revolutionary attitude towards women and sex. The relative freedom and affluence of the late 1940s and 1950s meant that families had raised children whose attitudes to work and leisure, parental authority and rights were significantly more liberal than those of their parents. They were growing up in a time of plenty; for the first time children were given status in their own right. Sexuality was freely spoken of, and the contraceptive pill liberated women in a way their parents found revolutionary.

To many men, brought up during the Depression, who had fought in the war and worked hard all their lives, believed in the sanctity of marriage, the value of a regular wage and their role as head of the household, what became known as the 'counterculture' was an affront. How dared these young people enjoy unbridled freedom without responsibility!

Times were good, education was more freely available than ever, consumerism was king. But in order to acquire the benefits of a labour-saving lifestyle, many more women had to join the workforce. Time payments for the good things in life could not be met from one wage; men whose egos depended on being the sole breadwinner saw this need of women to work as an affront to their masculinity. They worried that people would think they couldn't support their families.

And for wives and mothers who went into the workforce, an additional battle needed to be fought: Who would help with the housework? There had to be renegotiation, questioning of the status quo. This was the beginning of a process of enforced change that permanently altered men's relationships with their women and childen.

It is now clear that the global media network had a profound influence on Australians' aspirations and attitudes. Our rate of acquiring gadgetry is one of the highest in the world, and our acquisition of TV sets was no exception. Visual access to American culture gave us the best and the worst of their values. The soaps and the situation comedies extended the Hollywood fantasies that had become so familiar to movie-goers. But the other side of the picture was bleak: for the first time, non-combatants were able to see war — the Vietnam War — in all its dreadful detail. The dead could no longer be draped in the national flag under the cloaks of patriotism, idealism and populist slogans. Men and their aggression, heroics, mortality, fears, were now really exposed. And ordinary people could identify with their counterparts in other parts of the world in a much more immediate way. One picture truly was worth a thousand words.

For better or for worse, Australian men and women

had joined the great melting pot of global television. They also saw new and revolutionary things. For the first time, activists — black, anti-war, women — were on the march, insisting on being noticed. No longer were Australians safe in their isolation.

And for the first time, largely because of the American example presented over television, Australian men had to take notice of the ways in which women were beginning to blur the boundaries between male and female roles. Mateship, men's self-perception and their understanding of their role in society were about to change forever.

PART TWO

THE FEMINIST REVOLUTION AND ITS IMPACT ON MEN

The men marry us, keep us and our children; give us allowances, buy life insurance, and leave us their money and even hand us alimony! But all for one reason, and one reason alone. To buy us off! They don't want us running the world; they are willing to pay a lot, so they can run it themselves.

Christina Stead, *Letty Fox: Her Luck*

'WHAT DOES THIS HAVE DO WITH ME?'

Australian women have rarely been treated seriously, so it was not to be expected that a demand for their liberation would evoke a serious response. But if we are to try to end this habit of not heeding women's voices then it is important to insist on stating the meaning of what we are fighting for, and to fight to have that meaning taken seriously.

Anne Summers, *Damned Whores and God's Police*

The feminist movement, which began in the late 1960s and really hit Australia in the early 1970s, was to challenge the basic rationale of male/female relationships in a way they had never been challenged before. The whole weight of social, political, philosophical and religious thought was up for re-examination from a new perspective — women's.

In hindsight, it is possible to see where this impetus came from, and to accept it as inevitable. The generation growing up after the Second World War, the so-called 'baby boomers', came into a world of unparalleled prosperity. During the 1950s, most Western economies were stable and expanding. There was more money for education than there had ever been: more university places, more scholarships. And for the first time large numbers of women were becoming better educated, able to participate fully in opportunities that until now had been largely only available to men.

There was one other major factor that added to the impetus for change. In the early 1960s the contraceptive pill gained wide acceptance and use. It was cheap, it was readily available, and above all it was reliable. Women were now able to control their fertility more easily than at any time in human history. And because sex, marriage and having children no longer formed an inevitable progression, many more choices became available.

These factors — prosperity, the consumer revolution, greater availability of education and the freedom provided by the Pill — united to make women question and rebel against a great number of assumptions that both they and men had taken for granted. Like other Western women, most Australians had been taught that marriage and motherhood were the pinnacles of their lives, and their deepest satisfaction lay in fulfilling these roles. Of course, not all women had accepted this, but unless they had private means and/or a lot of determination, they found great difficulty in surviving in a male-dominated world; men earned money, women generally didn't. Traditionally, marrying a 'good provider' was what women did, after which they settled down, had children and looked after them.

Women knew that they were intelligent, aware human beings who were certainly able to contribute to society on a wider basis than simply as 'Brian's wife and Jenny's Mum', living in suburban houses and spending their days doing dreary housework. Being a wife and mother just didn't seem enough: many women felt trapped, without the capacity to make choices for themselves, caught in a system not of their making. This 'problem that has no name' was brilliantly articulated by Betty Friedan in *The Feminine Mystique*. This was one of the seminal books of the feminist revolution, read by large numbers of women in the mid 1960s. It was followed by a flood of others (two of the most influential being Germaine Greer's *The Female Eunuch* and Kate Millett's *Sexual Politics*) confirming that women had been imprisoned by male-dominated institutions, both sexual and social, for thousands of years. Many of these books also pointed out that women had been diminished by male-inspired gender stereotypes and expectations: a woman was supposed to be a whore in the bedroom, a gracious hostess in the dining room and a dear little housewife and mum the rest of the time. But now, if women worked together — *sisterhood is powerful* — and sought to challenge male power structures, both in the home and in the workplace, they had the capacity to change society, to change their world.

It is difficult to recapture the raw, urgent anger that many women expressed during the early years of the feminist movement. Years — possibly centuries — of frustration and stifled rebellion were finding a voice for the first time. And so much of it was directed against men, the agents of their oppression.

Phrases such as 'agent of oppression' affronted and bewildered the men hearing them for the first time. What did these women mean, oppression? Australian women weren't oppressed. They weren't living in poverty and starving to death; they weren't being imprisoned for their political or religious beliefs; they weren't like the Blacks in America, ground down and discriminated against. What did they mean, 'equality of opportunity'? Nothing was stopping them getting exactly what they wanted. They had most of it, anyway.

Husbands tended to say about their wives 'I wouldn't mind having her life; all she has to do is stay home all day chatting to the neighbours and watching TV if she wants to. She doesn't have to go to work, not like I do. Why would she want to change? She's got it made.' Employers were likely to say about women employees

'Well, she goes on about equal work for equal pay, and in theory that's fair enough, I suppose, but she's attractive and in about five years' time she'll get married and get pregnant and leave. So why should I invest money and effort in training her?'

Most men literally couldn't understand what women were on about. They were unable to take in the injustices being exposed by the women's movement, and to reconcile them with their own experiences of themselves. The average Aussie bloke didn't hit his wife, or rape other women. He didn't want his wife to be a slave. He could accept the need to correct injustice and free the oppressed, but the whole feminist business often seemed to him like the indulgence of middle-class overeducated women with nothing better to do.

The media didn't help; the issues were often trivialised, reduced to images of women burning bras. Very few men read feminist books, so they weren't entirely *au fait* with the arguments. And if they tried to discuss them with women, both sides became so heated that quarrels often ensued. They weren't even using the same language. For centuries, men had refined and used the language of logic, of the mind: this had become the language of power, expressing the view that the world of things was superior to the world of feelings. Now women were confirming the legitimacy of their own perspective by using the language of emotion, leaving men floundering and angry, and unable to comprehend. It's not really surprising that they failed to get the message.

Men found themselves being attacked for who they were, rather than for what they did as men. Not only did they generally fail to understand the issues, but they used male tactics of logic and reason to try and counteract what was a complex web of issues involving style, attitude and feelings — as well as justice. In this contest for hearts and minds, men were ill-prepared. A man might ask 'Why are we arguing about equality when we share everything

I earn, when we don't go without, and I never say you can't go out?' and be amazed and hurt if his wife saw that as a perfect example of why she felt patronised and unequal. She was being illogical, that was all. She had no idea what she wanted. In short, he was baffled by being presented with a situation that did not respond to his problem-solving skills. Another cornerstone of his identity was being undermined.

Male chauvinist pig is a phrase coined by feminists to describe the conservative reactionary male: the men who believed that the best form of defence was attack. These men's assertions about the natural and inevitable right of men to dominate women did much to heighten the awareness of other men to the issues of feminism. These M.C.Ps forced many men to take a position *vis-à-vis* feminism. Whilst many men embraced the fiercely anti-feminist slogans, many more were unwilling to identify with their aggressive position and took a neutral or pro-feminist stancc

In addition, some women weren't comfortable with some feminist ideas; they found they were expected to show solidarity with their sisters whose ideas they found alarmingly anti-male. Nevertheless, many arguments between men and women rapidly became expressions of extreme positions. Men's attempt to justify themselves was seen by women as women-bashing (akin to rape and other violence) and women's arguments were considered men-bashing. Man's inability to understand the profound nature of the revolution he was witnessing led to a self-fulfilling prophecy. The more men failed to take seriously the criticism of their hold on power, the more they reinforced women's justification for their discontent.

'IF MY VALUES ARE UNACCEPTABLE, WHAT DO I REPLACE THEM WITH?'

What the hell do these women want . . . blood?

I feel as though I'm being saddled with all the sins of the last twenty generations of men.

One of the features of the feminist revolution presented men as acting collectively, conspiring to decide and degrade the status of women. But as many men and women would argue, this is far from the truth.

Men's power and the institutions that supported them did not form a global plan of repression, consciously evolved and implemented. They developed from the essence of male socialisation which is competitive. Men find great difficulty in bonding together, even in small groups, for any length of time without finding other groups with whom to compete and at the same time competing with each other. As they saw it, the power that formed male institutions was — naturally — theirs by birthright. It always had been. For centuries men's psychological health had been based on a powerful self-image, underpinned by their central role in society. And whatever women thought of them, they were secure in their self-concept.

But now, large numbers of men were becoming

alienated in the very places where they had sheltered all their lives — in the home and the workplace. And their model of solidarity, mateship, wasn't working any longer. Traditionally, as we have said, mateship flourished against an external threat such as poverty, unemployment, invasion, the law, bosses. At times of external threat, a man could feel good about himself by fulfilling the role expectations that gave him status. He could fight, go on strike, join up — all active things that would make him feel proud of himself, and his family, in turn, proud of him.

But the issues raised by the feminist movement were *not* external in this way. They demanded self-criticism, examination of feelings, and a lot of other non-logic-based things that men had, traditionally, little stomach for. They weren't used to examining their feelings and motives, particularly not in front of women: it made them too vulnerable. They were called upon to use emotions they hardly acknowledged they possessed. For generations, they had been schooled to suppress feelings. Men were doers: give them a problem to solve or a job to do and they were fine. But here was something altogether different. Not only did they fail to understand the problem — they had no experience in the use of the tools that were needed to address it. How could they, when they themselves were the problem? It is very difficult to be empathic when you are being shot at.

Social behaviour that had been perfectly okay became suddenly unacceptable. Little courtesies such as opening car doors for women were likely to be greeted with glares and accusations of sexism instead of smiles and thanks: and men didn't know when to expect what. Some women laughed at their jokes, others found them patronising. For the first time, women were becoming frighteningly unpredictable.

Most difficult of all, perhaps, was the fact that for the first time men started feeling guilt by association. How could they possibly defend their gender, their maleness, themselves, without seeming tacitly to approve of rape or wife bashing?

Men hadn't any idea what to do about all this. If they reacted in the traditional way of males under threat — closing ranks and fighting back — they alienated the women in their lives, the very people on whom they relied for sustenance and support. In past battles, women had been the supply column that kept the troops alive. But not any more . . . women had become the threat from within.

It was, then, almost inevitable that men experienced the onslaught on their power base as an attack on their selfhood. Feminist criticism exposed the model they had used to define their lives, their values, as being largely negative. And so they became confused, vulnerable and prey to self-doubt.

It is often stated that Australia's divorce rate during the 1970s massively increased because of the introduction of the Family Law Act, pioneered by the late Lionel Murphy as Labor attorney-general. While the new grounds for divorce (irreconcilable breakdown of a marriage, no fault being apportioned) certainly had an impact, of equal significance was the dissatisfaction of many women with the quality of their marriages and the couple's lack of flexibility in being able to cope with the changes needed. This may sound like a plea for marriage at any price, but it simply acknowledges that a great many marriages went to the wall because both partners felt unable to make the kinds of changes that would cause them to be fulfilled and happy.

Part of the problem for many men was their lack of awareness of the *benefits* that could accrue from a more equal relationship. They didn't see it as a trade-off: how could they? They were in completely new, uncharted territory. And women were unable to tell men what was in it for them, too — that an equal relationship would give them more choice in their lives. Many of the front runners in the women's movement were apt to say: 'It's not up to us to tell you what's in it for you. We're all about meeting our own needs. For far too long we've worried about meeting yours. Now it's time for you to look after yourselves.' This response, though valid and necessary, was a partial view.

Selling these benefits was, in fact, probably one of the hardest marketing jobs ever tackled, and it was being done by women with little training in the selling field. Small wonder men didn't run to close the deal.

What is starting to become evident is that we can no longer ignore the interrelatedness and interdependence of men and women. Men can't get away from women, or vice versa, and in the final analysis we have to deal with one another because we *need each other.*

There is an enormous discrepancy between the public perception and the private reality of men's experience, and this gulf must be urgently addressed; it is central to the relationship between men and women. Without a shared reality, men and women, operating from different frames of reference, cannot hope to find a common purpose.

In a 1990 paper entitled 'The Role of the Father', Dr Don Edgar of the Australian Institute of Family Studies revealed some alarming data about men's self-concept.

Only 7 per cent of fathers agreed with the statement 'I take a positive attitude towards myself'. To the statement 'I feel that I am a person of worth, at least on an equal plane with others', 2 per cent of fathers strongly agreed, and 90 per cent disagreed. To 'I am able to do most things as well as other people' 11 per cent of fathers agreed, and only 4 per cent agreed with 'I generally have confidence that when I make plans I will be able to carry them out'.

Dr Edgar continued:

> There were very few differences between teenagers and their

parents on religion, on politics, on the use of authority and so on, but there were these incredible differences in self-esteem, self-image and self-confidence. The young kids were facing life fairly optimistically, the dads were in middle age, their marriage was often going sour, their jobs were often going sour, they were going through mid-life crisis.

Clearly, renegotiation — of roles, of attitudes, of expectations — had to occur. But how?

Because of their uncertainty, men look for a lead from the women in their lives, hoping to get clues about the kinds of people they are expected to be. This may seem a ridiculous statement, yet many women know that the need for reassurance is concealed behind the role of Lord and Master of the Universe. Women will recognise the validity of this assertion when they think of such things as: the job that must be inspected and praised by every member of the family five times; the expectation of thanks for doing something around the house that women do as a matter of course; the sulking — all are telling the man *I am valuable*.

Only in the 1990s can we men begin to see the long-term benefits that result from women having more choices. For the first time, men are able to consider their own choices. Do they want to be the primary breadwinners? Do they like being responsible for the mechanical things around the house, or would they rather cook or sew? As soon as we question the gender basis of roles, we open a Pandora's box of possibilities for both sexes. Although some aspects of the social upheaval that feminism brought have been slow to change, some male attitudes to the feminist revolution can be illustrated by the following case example. Though extreme, it highlights some of the dilemmas feminism gave rise to.

In 1969, Bob White was a senior clerk in the public service. He and his family lived in Hurstville, a southern suburb of Sydney. Neil and Jane were still at school, and Bob and his wife, Meg, had high hopes that the children would go to university. Bob and Meg were paying off their house, a three-bedroom weatherboard, had a late model car and had managed to rent a cottage down the south coast for the past few years for a week's holiday. Money was tight, particularly with the kids growing into teenagers and needing fashionable clothes.

Meg had a part-time job for a company which manufactured children's clothes. She enjoyed the work and the money it provided, and was proud that she could say to herself (only to herself because she knew Bob wouldn't understand) that her wages had bought the new fridge and given them all a holiday. These were much more useful and tangible things than cooking or cleaning the floor for the tenth time in a day. Meg worked three days per week, more if necessary. Her boss, Max, did not overpay her, but she knew how valuable she was, and Max knew that she knew.

Bob and Meg had a mutual understanding. When she was working, she would work out the menu for the next evening's meal and prepare what could be done beforehand; the rest was left to the kids to prepare when they came home from school. If they forgot, and Meg was working late, Bob and the kids would sit down to dinner late, at 7.30 or 8 p.m., and Bob would sulk. This wasn't his idea of family life; getting home from work and having to do cooking when he got home. He didn't want to hold Meg back, and he liked the money she earned, but was it worth it? He could no longer stay back and have a beer at the club, he had to be home to supervise the kids. He didn't tell the other blokes the truth, just made feeble excuses and felt resentful. None of this was ever discussed directly, it just simmered below the surface.

Max's business was growing and he decided to open another factory. He asked Meg if she would manage the present one for him on a full-time basis. Having trusted her with the books for seven years, he knew she was reliable, got on well with the other staff and wouldn't put up with any nonsense. He was much more confident that she could do the job than she was.

Bob's initial reaction was surprise and some disbelief. He could never see Meg as anything more than a part-time bookkeeper as well as a wife and mother and the idea that she could be in charge of an organisation was a new one. Not that he didn't believe that she could do it, it had just never occurred to him that anyone would put so much confidence in his Meg.

After some disruption to their routine, the Whites adapted reasonably well. Meg gained in confidence and their finances improved. Soon Meg was earning more than Bob. He told himself that this didn't really matter, but nevertheless felt hurt when she would buy things for the house without consulting him first; they had always planned major purchases together. He felt a curious mixture of resentment, frustration and admiration. There never seemed to be time for relaxing any more. The evenings were spent getting dinner and clearing up, getting the kids organised, fixing the lunches for the following day and both Bob and Margaret would fall into bed usually too tired for sex.

Bob felt that he was dealing with forces and issues outside his knowledge and control. He didn't want to hold Meg back as she was doing so well, but he looked back nostalgically to a time when they might have been poorer but at least he knew where he stood and felt valuable because of the family's obvious need for his leadership.

Jane was secretly proud of her mother, but outwardly resentful of the extra chores she herself had to do. Her recently graduated English teacher held firm views on the status of women and Jane found the debates in the classroom very stimulating. When she took home her new-found beliefs about the status of women, her father would immediately respond, 'What would you know?' The arguments would usually escalate till her mother would step in and tell Jane to stop arguing with her father. Bob saw this as Meg taking his side and felt supported in his anti-feminist stance, little knowing that Meg felt proud of her daughter and was starting to feel embarrassed by Bob's overbearing response to his daughter's new-found insights.

Neil was bemused by all this. His temperament was closer to his mother's than his father's. He didn't argue as his sister Jane did, and often watched, in a detached way, the endless conflicts between his sister and his father. Why did she bother? Nothing would ever change Dad's view, couldn't she see that?

These family rows were good for Jane. They taught her debating tactics, refined her arguments, gradually taught her to use less emotion and more logic. She topped her year in English and went on to university to study political science.

Being the younger of the two, Neil missed his mother a lot when she first began full-time work. He had been used to talking with her when he came home from school; she'd help him with his homework and let him help with the cooking, which he loved. She seemed a friend as much as a mother. He could tell her anything and she would listen, not like his father, who would have an opinion or solution on offer before you had stated the problem. He loved his father but didn't know or understand him. So when his mother started full-time work, Neil became withdrawn, feeling deprived of his mother but unable to talk to his father.

Bob tried his best to accept the changes being forced on him and the family, but it was hard. His daughter no longer respected him; she never had a pleasant word to say to him. Whatever he said, no matter how trivial, was scrutinised, analysed and thrown back at him. Home was no longer a haven or sanctuary, it was a battlefield. He never knew what to say to Neil, either. They seemed to have very little in common. Bob tried to bring his son out of himself, knowing that he missed closeness with his mother, but most of his attempts failed. (Neither he nor Neil could know that the ease of relating between mother and son was the product of a lifetime's connectedness and could not be manufactured overnight, despite the assertions of the television advertisements.)

Bob got on with daily life, as did the rest of the family. At times he was tempted to chuck it all in, leave the state, go north, encouraged by a workmate who was herself unhappy. She was twenty-seven and had had only one serious relationship in the past five years. She found him appealing because of his stability and gentleness. They had a brief affair, but he got cold feet and she lost interest.

Bob and Meg are still married. Neil is married to an older woman who was divorced with two children. He is a computer programmer who works from home and helps with the children. Jane lectures in political science, was briefly married to a journalist who turned out to be violent, so she left him. Now she is not sure she wants to marry again but she hates the loneliness of being single.

There is nothing dramatic or even notable about the White family — but then perhaps that's the nature of change as seen at the family level. It generally involves small tensions, a little shift, new ways of doing things — not because of a new philosophy but because they work, because people ask for change or demand it. On the face of it, then, no members of the White family benefited from the feminist movement, but in reality growth is about increasing options, so what they lost in harmony they more than made up for in choices. They would all be more able to break out of traditional roles. And, while Bob has reaped the least benefit of all from the change, he may have the insight to see how beneficial it could be for his children.

When a family struggles to cope with major social

upheaval they have the potential to grow from the experience or, by failing to confront it, disintegrate. Bob's family grew. If we define conflict as negative, then the tensions within their family were undoubtedly painful at the time, but if we see conflict as the inevitable consequence of difference, then we can start to see the positive aspects of the family's struggle. Flexibility was introduced, the women grew in stature and self-confidence, the men learned about choices.

It's naive to believe that change comes about easily. It's important to remember that often the struggle is commensurate with the rewards. A man in Bob's situation today could be better able to cope with the different aspirations within the family because of these earlier struggles.

The impact of feminism changed society for ever. The changes brought by the feminist movement go right across the board — from awareness of sexism in speech to equal pay for women. And, as we have seen, they have had a huge impact on men.

PART THREE
MALE IDENTITY: LEARNING HOW TO BE A MAN

If I were to emulate my father, I'd have no marriage. He was and still is a male chauvinist pig. So far as I'm concerned, it's all new ground. We're learning as we go.

It is impossible to look at Australian men and mateship today, without first examining how they develop an identity. To do this, we need to consider society's influence through certain role models and expectations.

Role models are important to us all. It is a universal human need to seek the example of somebody whom we consider more powerful, wiser, more heroic perhaps, than we are ourselves. Our degree of self-esteem plays an enormous part in how we identify with these role models. Those lacking self-value will find it difficult to believe that they can attain such lofty heights as their heroes. However, if the target for emulation is set too high for someone's real or perceived capabilities, the outcome is inevitable disappointment and a reduction of self-esteem. We often see this with teenagers. The 'you can do it if you try' motivation is fine when the motivator is aware of the teenager's potential, and the external motivation of the teacher or coach is matched by the teenager's own self-belief. But if it is not, if the goal is regarded by the teenager as being unattainable, the choice of role model may change: the teenager may choose an anti-hero as a role model.

FATHERS

> I'm not the man my father wanted me to be. I don't feel complete, I'll never be what he would have respected. I always feel cornered by his expectations.

For most of us, our first role models are our parents. They have a very powerful impact on the goals and values we set for our lives. The extent to which we follow our parents' lead, consciously or unconsciously, depends on many things — not least, our own view of them as parents. We may be determined to avoid the pitfalls of our parents' style of child rearing ('no kid is going to have to suffer what I did'), and only want to reproduce those things we believed were positive or valuable. Unfortunately, choosing the positive aspects of our role models is a lot harder than we think. Often those traits we try to extinguish in bringing-up our children are the very ones that come back to haunt us. One expression — among many — that is likely to lead relationships into shark-infested waters is 'You're just like your father/mother,' to somebody whose greatest fear is that he or she will end up mirroring the behaviour they most disliked in their parents.

For men, the obvious primary role model is the father. The problem here is that often fathers are mostly absent, either in reality or emotionally. Traditionally, fathers have been rather stern, remote figures, the last court of appeal for discipline ('you wait till your father gets home'). In most families, the mother is the primary nurturer. And so male children are presented with a problem from the outset.

One of the great hurdles we have in establishing identity is to differentiate ourselves and to separate from the primary care-giver. Girls can establish an identity before they separate by copying their mothers, but boys have a much harder task; they have to be different from their mothers in order to gain independence. They have to leave the security of the nurturing mother before they have a clear picture of what a man is.

When we look at adolescent males, we can see why so many of them adopt an aggressive style in addition to their biological imperatives: they act tough because they are frightened inside and uncertain in their role. When a boy makes tentative moves towards independence and self-determination , he is usually encouraged by his parents, who see him becoming a man. The power that is seen as a male's right by birth means that he is less likely to be challenged than his sister.

Consequently, many boys grow up too soon: their early muscle flexing is regarded as being a sign of maturity, and their early flights from the nest are seen as their capability to fly solo. Too often, young men find themselves weaned before they can feed themselves. They may find themselves, figuratively speaking, standing outside the house saying 'I don't want to go, I'm scared, I didn't expect you to take me seriously.'

(Fathers are further discussed in Part 4, *Men After Feminism*, under the section 'The Family Man' at page 76.)

HEROES

> How do you survive and be authentic? It's bloody hard to be all that you are expected to be and live.

Our secondary role models are our gods and heroes. It is very doubtful whether any society can have a collective identity without first producing images of the people whose values have been shaped by great deeds: the gods of the ancient world were generally the unattainable models who shaped the values of those societies. They were invented by men, in order to help people gain mastery over their environment, and to make sense and order out of chaos. Ordinary mortals could aspire only to rise above themselves, to be better than they were. While they could not be gods, they could at least emulate those who stood above the crowd.

Australian men seem to have a great empathy for the tragic hero; perhaps it is so close to their own fears that they can easily empathise through identification. Few men see themselves as successful — most believe that as individuals they have little power to influence their own lives significantly. The early bushrangers provided the anti-hero role models which gave short-term hope, but offered no long-term solution. Men carry a collective culture of heroic failure: Ned Kelly, Gallipoli, the swaggie in 'Waltzing Matilda', Breaker Morant, the soldier settlers. We have come to value the struggle more than the success. 'Waltzing Matilda' should have been our national anthem, as it embodies all of the elements of the cultural hero: fearlessness, hardship, contempt for authority and a loser.

Mateship flourishes against adversity, be it war or an oppressive authority. To be successful in overcoming these things would remove the adversity, and thus the need for mateship would be diminished. If an ordinary man achieved success, though he may not join the oppressor, he would no longer belong to the battlers — and alienation is not a positive alternative to mateship. Mateship is thus perpetuated, along with the 'ideal' Australian male qualities it embodies, including toughness and a disdain for 'weak' emotion.

Following the example of contemporary heroes — actors, politicians, industrialists, sports stars — as models of behaviour, however, is often fraught with danger. Those who rise high enough above the crowd to be seen are rarely complete people: often the very process that elevates can also distort. The image of the high flyer is generally one-dimensional — portraying people whose success has been purchased at the price of their wholeness. So much of their emotional, creative, financial and intellectual resources, so much of their time, needs to be devoted to their achievements that the rest of their lives become wastelands, or so it seems. And because their lives are played out on a public stage, they become the property of the public via the media.

Even if most of our contemporary role models are not cardboard cutouts — and I'm sure they can't all be — the media seem generally incapable of showing us more than one dimension. So we are left with role models in the public arena who are almost useless to us as blueprints for successful living — unless all we want from life is fame and fortune, or unless 95 per cent of us are content to see ourselves as failures!

The role models presented by the media have a profound effect on our self-confidence. At the flick of a switch, we can be entertained by the world's best in all fields: we have become armchair critics of the most exciting performances. And our instant society has led us to expect that our own performance will somehow compare with the people we see on television or read about.

A great deal has been written about the negative impact that the typical advertising model has on women. Generally speaking, they have been portrayed as sexy, vacuous, young, subordinate. Anyone with half an eye can see that most women cannot identify with this image. So powerful are these images, however, that many women feel inadequate because of their failure to measure up to them.

On the face of it, the situation seems better for men. The advertising industry has very cleverly picked on heroic, powerful and active images to represent men, and they use ordinary blokes. Images of men in the media, then, are generally positive. But the problem is, again, one of identification. In the media, men are doers or slobs, young and athletic, or handsome and successful. If they are old, they are very attractive, with silver hair (for instance, Sean Connery) or they are retired with loved ones around them, enjoying the fruits of their labours. (It is ironic, too, that the commercials that have made the greatest effort to depict ordinary working Aussies advertise beer, that other national symbol of manliness.)

The combination of these images gives men, like women, very little with which to identify. The soft, uncertain, tender, creative, loving, frightened part of men does not exist in the media. Men are rarely portrayed as nurturers; they are shown as bumbling idiots (for example in the movies *Kramer v Kramer* and *Three Men and a Baby*). If you believed the media, it would seem that men are incapable of carrying out the simplest domestic or nurturing tasks. What this does is make men feel inadequate about the nurturing, caring and sensitive part of their personalities.

WOMEN

> What really shits me off are the expectations women have of me. It wouldn't be so bad if there was some consensus, but they all seem to want something different.

Men generally find great difficulty in identifying themselves with some of the images that have come about as a result of the feminist movement. According to the stereotypical image, they stand accused as oppressors, rapists, wife beaters, self-interested morons, insensitive penis-driven clods, intolerant and heartless troglodytes. In the face of such onslaughts, men have found it almost impossible to stand still long enough to say 'I'm not all of these things, but what am I?' and 'Who do I want to be?' This process of redefinition pushes men to the limits of their own language. As a result, many became defensive and attacked back with unsuccessful attempts to reinforce their own stand. Just as they found great difficulty in coming to terms with the underlying philosophy of the women's movement because they lacked the language of emotions and the skills of self-awareness, so they are now being impoverished by these same shortcomings.

We cannot really know whether men's longing for new directions and identity is solely the result of the women's movement and the resultant upheaval, or whether it is partly a product of the twentieth-century blues: general disillusionment with our own lives as a result of global uncertainty and, particularly for men, the alienation experienced as a result of their work taking them away from the home. Men feel an emptiness that is hard to define: they are starting to know what they *don't* want and, while this is a starting point, it is hardly a blueprint for change. The need for relationships that meet our basic needs for love and a sense of belonging are even more urgent now than they ever were. In a world that is becoming increasingly alienating and impersonal, this hunger for intimacy, stability and trust becomes an all-consuming drive.

It is at this point that men are faced with one of the essential paradoxes of their lives. Whose mirror should they use in order to see themselves? Women's or men's?

What about women's? Many men feel that women's definition of being a man is too critical, lacking empathy or positive direction. Negative feedback demoralises rather than promotes growth and change, and provides no positive vehicle for the progress of men.

As women move into the higher echelons of the workforce, they often seem to become trapped in the same rat race that men have been experiencing for years. While we may believe all the arguments that say this is inevitable, the fact remains that women's entry into these areas of society has not resulted in any profound change to that society. Women seem to have become absorbed into the same networks of the patriarchal society they once so strongly objected to. So often men find women demand incomprehensible things of them — or that they have the same problems as men do in the workforce.

In reality, women's attitudes to men in general are less influential than men's perception of those attitudes. If men think that women will be angry with them, or critical, that belief will determine their future actions no matter what the reality of the perception. Men will, and do, act defensively, uncertain of their reaction. A man will ask 'How can I be a strong, decisive person (women hate wimps) and a sensitive, caring person (women like them)?' For most men this is too difficult, the task too exacting. They will probably expect women to be angry and critical, even when individual experience contradicts this expectation. A man may say to himself 'I bet whenwe get married she'll change and start being nagging and critical.'

Because of the power imbalance between men and women, women will generally take men on their own valuation, rarely questioning the validity of a man's assertion or self-concept. This lack of challenge leaves men uncertain, incomplete, with no choice but to believe in their own hype. What is interesting about this, is that despite women's private experience of men, which frequently contradicts the popular stereotype, women collectively reinforce this negative view for themselves and for men. It is as if women have to believe the popular stereotype because it is universally reinforced: in the media and elsewhere. In this sense, women are as much influenced by ideas of 'what it means to be a man' as are men themselves. We have here the well-known phenomenon of the Emperor's new clothes. What woman will say, 'Men aren't like that, and I don't necessarily want a man who is'?

MATES

> All the bullshit about mates. I've got mates but no friends. I'd no more dream of showing them my real self than fly. We all know it's a facade, but go along with it. I'd love to have a real friend.

Well, what about men getting together to reinforce their own identity? Of course men get together, but this is usually for a specific outwardly-directed purpose — to watch the Test cricket or the football Grand Final together in the pub, for instance. None of this challenges the concept of mateship. But there is a newly emerging men's movement, partly concerned with remythologising and re-imagining what it means to be a man. It is described in books such as *Iron John* by the American Robert Bly. The most common theme in this search for identity seems to be the great outdoors — men go camping together, being self-sufficient and comradely, and expressing pent-up emotions that reveal a longing for closeness and vulnerability. Then the camp ends and they all go home. Are they changed? Are things different for them?

Well, it's an instant solution — but like most of those, it doesn't work for very long: providing immediate solutions to fundamental problems is usually impossible. The belief that beating a drum, carrying a spear or a stick and sitting by a bonfire — behaving like a Navajo or an Apache, representative of a culture that evolved over thousands of years in a quite different context — will put modern middle class (usually American) men in touch with the essence of their lives is not only naive but extraordinarily arrogant. If men are to succeed in participating in the way our society evolves, we shall have to look deeper and farther than periodic role playing by small groups of middle class American men.

It is important not to dismiss these 'bonding' attempts out of hand because they serve a purpose in several ways. Firstly, it is better to do something than nothing: at least you learn what works and what doesn't. Secondly, some of them show that men are looking for a new form of self-expression, a new honesty. But you don't achieve intimacy by ordering people to unburden themselves and be vulnerable. These changes need to be nurtured if they are to become part of men's daily repertoire. The nursery must be as close to real life as possible if the changes are to survive the transfer from embryo to healthy growth. The more hothouse the environment in which the new plant is germinated, the less its survival potential.

The theme that seems to be emerging is man's isolation from his own creativity, his spontaneity. The standard adult male role leaves little room for this: if alienation is the most pressing problem for men — from themselves, from each other and from women — more money, more relationships and more satisfying jobs are not likely to be the answers. As a group, men need to look for new resources to point them in new directions. Their close identity with what they do for a living, which is the major source of ego support, is the area of men's lives which is perhaps the most difficult to change: it carries the greatest threat of loss of identity. If I am what I do, then I tamper with what I do at great risk to myself.

If creativity, connection with our emotions and spirituality are needed, men may find inspiration in the universal vehicles of self-expression — music, dance, writing, painting, singing and other forms of the arts. Throughout history, symbols of societies' identity have been constantly reinforced through ritualised play. Dance and song became the channels through which men expressed their joy and sorrow, and these songs and dances are the living history books that connect the generations. Major events are, and always have been, experienced within the context of music and dance — these have been central to the event, not incidental.

But, of course, the early history of Australia was hardly conducive to displays of singing and dancing. Life as a convict didn't leave much opportunity for it and, more than likely, the only dancing seen was a mate at the end of a rope. Certainly things loosened up as the century wore on and people had greater leisure, but even today Australian males have a great fear of making fools of themselves by dancing and singing. We only seem to be able to achieve a sense of fearless self-expression when we are drunk. As one member of my group said 'The louder we get, the more we are hiding something real behind the silliness'.

This need for self-expression may also explain a common complaint women have that men are childish. A wife may say, typically, 'He is just like the kids' or 'I have three children, not two and a husband.' Either such women are unobservant of their husband's behaviour, or men really do feel the need to express themselves in childlike ways; men often feel trapped in the adult male role that leaves so little room for spontaneous play. Maybe women feel threatened by behaviour that exposes the hunter/defender as wanting to put away his sword and helmet and go out to play. Most would agree, however, that men find it difficult to let their hair down and just *be*. Their need to achieve, to compete, seems to be overwhelming; life seems to need to be purposeful, and even leisure is contrived so that there is an outcome.

If men are impoverished and isolated from the mainstream of their emotional energy and flexibility, then their leaders are doubly so: too often change requires those in power to give ground, which means that our institutional leaders will propose changes that affect almost everything but their own positions of power and dominance.

I can hear people saying that this is all a lot of hogwash and asking whether I expect men to become basketweavers who sing and dance in the streets. Of course not. Singing and dancing will hardly transform men overnight into the kinds of people many yearn to be.

However, I am arguing strongly for men to stop repressing their emotions. The repression of emotional expression can be compared to trying to drown a tennis ball: no matter how many times it is pushed down, it keeps bobbing up. And there is a clear correlation between stress and emotional repression. The greater the repression, the greater the effort required to keep the lid on, the more the pressure builds up, the greater the stress.

There is also a direct correlation between self-expression and self-value. As I have already said, basing your self-concept on your job, on achievement, material success, does not mean, at a fundamental level, that you feel good about yourself. (Why, then, is it necessary for people to keep wanting to achieve bigger and better things in order to feel valuable and lovable?) The correlation between self-expression and self-value lies at a deeper level of awareness, and is predicated on the conviction that 'I am who I am' not 'I am what I do'. If one can find acceptance when expressing the unexpurgated edition of oneself, including just playing or even being silly, relationships are more likely to be honest and intimacy will be more likely to result.

Singing and dancing won't give men intimacy in their relationships, but they may be a small start in their finding out who they are.

As we can see, uncertainty and insecurity are the major characteristics underpinning the Australian male. Until men are able to develop role models which display variety and richness, they will continue to be beset by unrealistic stereotypes and self-doubt.

PART FOUR
MEN AFTER FEMINISM

For me, the issue is without definition. I can't look back for ideas, I don't like my present role and I can't get a clear picture of the future.

Australian society in the 1990s is markedly different from that of the 1960s which spawned the feminist movement. Men can no longer be grouped together under one definition. The revolution of the past thirty years has expanded the range of choices for men as never before. Men can now be gay and proud, sensitive New Age, traditional or still searching for an identity. The old strait-jackets that held men within rigidly defined parameters have been progressively loosened.

The women's movement spawned and encouraged other oppressed groups to organise and declare their determination to obtain a better deal.

The gay liberation movement was to challenge both the attitude of society to homosexuality and the definition of masculinity. Gay men have, by their determination to be seen and heard, forced men to recognise that the hetro model of maleness is not the only one. The gay man's relationship with other men and his balancing a career with home-making, are both rich areas for the education of those hetro men who will be honest enough to look and learn.

The men's movement has spawned a range of ideas that attempt to address the diversity of men's emerging needs, namely the idea of the New Age man. Whilst these groups still represent a tiny percentage of the male population, they nevertheless give direction to men's aspirations. What they seem to have in common is a strong desire for men to develop a new self-awareness and sensitivity.

The sexual revolution has exposed the impoverishment of men's sexual expression. Both men and women are learning that the liberation of men has major advantages for everyone — and the area of sexuality is long overdue for change.

THE SEXUAL MAN

Men see coitus as the meat in the sandwich of fore-play and after-play; women see it as the icecream in a Bombe Alaska of intimate emotional exchange.

Beatrice Faust, *Women, Sex and Pornography*

How can you tell whether they want sex or not?

Thanks to the Victorians' denial of sexuality, both men and women have been left impoverished, trapped into narrow definitions that deny the rich variety of sexual appetites, methods of expression, and desires. There is probably no area in which men and women understand each other's needs so little.

The assumption that any group in society will have the same tastes and desires in one aspect of their lives would be seen as ridiculous if it were applied to any area except sex. We have enormous variety in our eating, sleeping, reading, sporting, educational and recreational habits, and nobody would think of suggesting that one food would satisfy all appetites. Our market-oriented society ensures that all tastes are catered for. Yet, when it comes to sex, all men (and women) are lumped together in an absurd presumption of sameness.

There is a link between men's sensitivity and their sexual performance. The insensitive macho man is less affected by his partner's attitude to him, secure in his own superiority and sexual performance. Sensitive men are more likely to be put off by negative feedback, sensitive men need sensitive partners in order to perform.

> When I feel pressure from my partner in general areas, it spills over into my sexual performance. The pressure from a woman causes me to stuff up.

Let's look at the stereotypes. Men are still shackled by too narrow a role expectation that presupposes that they have all been cast from the same mould at birth. By this universal definition, men are understood (and required) to be devoid of emotion in matters sexual. In other words, they are large, throbbing penises with nothing more than the desire to put it into a handy hole. Ask any group of women about men's sexuality and you are likely to have fed back the widely accepted negative view about men's sexual appetite and preoccupation with their genitals. (There is a women's joke that illustrates this: What is the definition of a man? A life support system for a penis.)

On the other hand, women have been expected to be passive, receptive, chaste and only fulfilled by a loving relationship. Their appeal to men is decided by their physical beauty and modest demeanour. Women have been presented with almost insuperable obstacles to natural sexual expression. It is no wonder that much of the female population has rebelled against such absurdly unrealistic expectations, and that the sexual revolution of the 1960s and 1970s took place. However, this is by no means invariable, of course: women brought up or accustomed to concealing their sexuality are likely to give deliberately ambiguous messages about their sexual needs.

When this is placed beside the man's primary message that he must be the hunter, the initiator, we have the ingredients for a great — even a classic — misunderstanding. Men have heard a lot of talk about women not knowing what they want: saying 'no' when they really mean 'yes', needing to be wooed, not responsible for their own arousal. So a man is likely to approach a sexual encounter with considerable apprehension: I know what I want, but what about her? Will my advances be responded to or rejected? If she seems reluctant, is it because she doesn't want to appear eager, or is it that she is not interested in me or in sex, or in sex with me? Careful of his image, a man will also consider the risk that other men present: 'The depth of man's sexuality in all encounters with women cannot be overemphasised. I check out the women and then the guys to see what the level of competition is from the men.'

The discrepancy between men's public image and private reality is best illustrated by this composite case example; the information has been drawn from my own counselling practice.

Forty-two-year-old John was married to Paula, aged thirty-nine. John came from a warmly happy family which was rather well-off; his father was a solicitor. Paula came from a working class background with five brothers and sisters. She was determined not to emulate her mother, whom she saw as hard and bitter and who, because of a strong Methodist background, considered all fun as evil.

John and Paula had two children in primary school. Both had jobs: John as a computer software salesman and Paula as a teacher. They had been married for ten years. They came to me for counselling because they felt they were drifting apart: Paula complained that John's working hours were too long and they never did anything together. He was unwilling to admit, at first, that anything was wrong.

When I asked what their sex life was like, an unfortunate but typical picture emerged. Both were sexually dissatisfied; sex happened very infrequently — perhaps once every three months, and even then it was largely unsatisfying. It wasn't as if each was the other's first sexual partner; John had been married before and divorced after three years, and both had experimented with different sexual partners when they were in their twenties (though both now regarded most of those experiences as rather empty). When they got together, sex was great fun for both of them, but after two or three years it settled into a routine that made every move and counter move predictable.

Her upbringing would not permit her to initiate sex, so John always had to make the first move. This meant that he often asked for sex when she did not want it, so he was refused far more often than he was accepted. They never talked much about what they liked or disliked, so John was never quite sure whether Paula meant 'no' or whether she was waiting to be aroused. Often, because of his efforts to 'turn on' Paula, John would become strongly aroused, and by the time it was clear from her behaviour that she wasn't particularly interested, he had quite an erection. His realisation that she didn't want him led to a strong sense of hurt and rejection on his part, and he would lie awake, going over in his head how often he had been refused sex in the past few weeks.

Sometimes, if Paula (who had to look after two primary school children as well as holding down her own job) didn't feel too tired, she would feel sorry for John and tell him that sex was fine, seeing he wanted it so badly. This made John very angry inside; it felt as if charity were being offered. He never knew whether to accept, just to ease his own frustration, or to refuse, just to show her that he had his pride. Paula knew little of these feelings; she was only aware that the next morning John was often in a bad mood before he went to work.

Paula, because of her upbringing, was unable to ask for sex when she wanted it. She gave out what she thought were clear signals of her desire — cooking his favourite meal, sitting beside him and asking him to talk to her instead of reading the paper, having a bath before going to bed early. But unfortunately most of these signals were interpreted only on a practical level. John (maddeningly) was apt to say 'I'll come to bed later when I've finished watching this program', or 'What a nice meal', or 'Look, I'd like to read this article in peace, I've had a hard day.'

By the time both had endured these crossed signals for some time, they felt undervalued. Paula felt neglected, married to a man who wanted sex only when it suited him, and who was insensitive to her needs. He thought he was married to a woman who was undersexed, insensitive and unaware of his deep sense of rejection.

Without any outside assistance, this situation would have been unlikely to change; their perceptions of each other were never corrected because they were not verbal. Both parties needed long-term counselling, first of all to change the distortions in their perceptions, and then to change their behaviours. The relationship blossomed.

The story of John and Paula indicates how easily misunderstandings about the nature of sexuality can grow and become serious. Both partners tend to see one another as much like themselves, but with different attachments designed to fit neatly together. This is not so.

Man and his relationship to his penis needs to be understood. Firstly, there is no direct link between the male will and the penis; a man cannot have an erection because he wants one any more than he can go to sleep because he wants to. In fact, there is an almost inverse relationship between desire and result (any man who has lain awake for hours trying to go to sleep will attest to that fact). The setting for sleep can be provided, just as can the stimulus for an erection, but if this does not happen, trying for an erection will lead to failure, which compounds the failure and makes attaining a successful erection less and less likely. Men are very well aware of this lack of control and vulnerability to erectile failure, so when they stake much of their ego on sexual performance they are playing a risky game that, like any high-risk investment, is capable of quick high-yield returns but also substantial long-term losses. However, at the same time it must be said that there exists a strong link between a man's self-image and his ability to get and hold an erection.

Whereas all a man's needs are focused on his penis, a woman's sensuality and sexual expression are diffused throughout her whole body. Women constantly complain that men as lovers are preoccupied with their vaginas. (Another women's joke: What is the difference between a pub and a clitoris? Nine out of ten Australian men can find their way to a pub.) They are likely to assume that a man's body is as attuned to touch as a woman's, a dangerous assumption.

A great many men have so lost touch with their need for physical non-sexual contact that the desire never surfaces in its original form; it has all been subsumed under the heading of 'sex'. Yet at the same time, men will say that they need a partner who is warm, loving and understanding as well as sexually satisfying. Their recognition of the little boy inside them who feels lonely, thrust into an adult world that is cold and demanding, is, however, largely non-existent. This being the case, it is hardly surprising that men are accused of being unaware and insensitive.

And they are then accused of always wanting to have sex. In many relationships, non-sexual touching is almost non-existent. Women complain that in the early stages of a relationship, physical contact such as holding hands and cuddling were often sufficient in themselves, they did not necessarily lead to sex, but later on almost all physical contact is expected to lead to the bedroom.

Men's inability to articulate their feelings in any way other than by action means that the most common vehicle for expression of affection and tenderness is sexual. This lack of articulation can lead a man into very narrow and dangerous places. Not only is sex frequently his major act of loving and tenderness, it also has to substitute for expression of most other emotions; fear, anxiety, hurt, loss, disappointment. No wonder men are confused in their sexual expression.

The essential differences between male and female sexuality can be illustrated by another case example.

Gillian was in her late thirties, married to Mark, a forty-year-old graphic designer. They had two school-age children, one of their own and one from Gill's previous marriage. Their sex life was infrequent and unrewarding — all the more galling, considering the early days of their relationship. When they started their sex life together, it was wonderfully satisfying to them both. They sometimes spent hours at foreplay, exploring each other's sensuality.

If we had been able to examine their individual experiences, however, we might have detected significant differences that were not outwardly apparent.

Mark saw himself as the initiator, to whom Gillian was responding. He was in control of a process whose logical and inevitable conclusion was his erect penis ejaculating in her vagina either during or after her climax. This was what he was giving her, because he loved her. He believed that she shared his view of the experience; he never even questioned that she might not have done.

But for Gill, their lovemaking had a different meaning, a significance that was markedly different from Mark's. Gill's experience of a bad marriage had left her with a sexual frustration that masturbation had done little to quell. And so she approached making love with Mark enthusiastically and with high anticipation. Yet her expectations were based on different needs. What Mark felt were the preliminaries were to Gill the main events. The sense of intimacy and care she received and gave during these long sessions were essential to her responsiveness. She wasn't responsive because she felt sexually aroused, she was responsive because she felt loved and valued as a woman. Her breasts and vagina were simply vehicles for this self-expression, not separate from her, and while she enjoyed sex, and felt fulfilled by it, for her it was as much giving as receiving.

If Gill had been asked whether she could do without talking, caressing, lovemaking or intercourse, she would have said the last; Mark, on the other hand, would have opted for the first three.

Gill and Mark never discussed these differences; both seemed to enjoy their time together, and both believed they felt the same way about it. Mark saw their early days of lovemaking as delightful, but also as a time of learning about each other; what each liked and disliked, what turned Gill on and what he could expect from her. His primary data gathering was about what kind of lover he was and what he could expect as a reward for his diligence and care. Believing that Gill was just like him, except that she had a vagina instead of a penis, he never understood what she regarded as primary and then secondary to her. For him, lovemaking was like any other learning experience: once you had done it a few times, you knew the essentials and could dispose with the manual and, as it were, take short cuts.

Their differences in attitude became problematical only when their baby was born. He took up all their spare time, and they were also often short of sleep. Gill and Mark were prepared for this, but in different ways. Gill was often stressed and tired, looking for emotional support, as was Mark — but each had a different way of giving and getting this.

Mark would say 'Why don't we leave this until morning

and get an early night?' (Male talk for sex). Gill would jump at the idea, taking him literally. When they got into bed, Gill would kiss Mark goodnight and he would start making unambiguous moves towards her. Gill was damned if she agreed, damned if she didn't. If she consented, she would feel used (and even more tired); if she refused, Mark would sulk for a day or two.

Mark was puzzled and angry, of course. Why was she rejecting him when he wanted to make love to her? Had she gone off sex, or off him? She had enjoyed it before: why not now? In his view, if time was at a premium, you cut out the preliminary bouts and went for the main event. Gill felt hurt: did he expect her to just feel like sex any time he did? Didn't he know how tired she was, how unsexy she felt?

Mark looked for complex reasons to simple problems: perhaps she had put on an act to trap him in the first place, perhaps having the baby had done something to her hormones, perhaps she was having an affair. This lack of understanding only made matters worse; when they did decide to have sex he would try harder to turn her on. So, without a word or a caress, he would try and excite her . . . and be surprised and hurt that it didn't achieve the desired result. When she told him to get it over with so they could get some sleep, that was the final straw. He didn't want to be where he wasn't welcome, so he went to sleep on the lounge.

Mark eventually met someone else whom he saw as more accommodating and willing to understand him, and he had an affair that eventually brought the whole matter to a head. As so frequently happens, it was the crisis that brought them into counselling and proved the catalyst for change. So often an affair is a symptom rather than a cause, and it needs to be treated as such.

Of course, both Gill and Mark misunderstood each other's main vehicle of sexual expression. Sadly, they are not unique in Australian society. Far from it, in fact.

THE FAMILY MAN

. . . for men, family life is part of an assumed background. It is just one stopping place in the landscape of experience.

Anne Summers, *Damned Whores and God's Police*

MARRIAGE

I feel confused about my role because I'm still expected to be the hunter/gatherer and the protector and I'm also expected to be 100 per cent more sensitive, intuitive and understanding than any man was ten years ago. Quite frankly, it pisses me off. We never seem to be quite clear on the expectations we have of one another in the relationship.

Australia has a very high marriage rate, which peaked in the 1970s and has been declining ever since. Why?

Well, one factor is that larger numbers of people are choosing to live together without marriage. Another is that men are becoming more reluctant to tie the knot than women.

Again, why? If, as some women believe, marriage was invented almost solely for the benefit of men, why should men be so reluctant to go into it? And they seem to be: one often hears women in their thirties lamenting the fact that there seem to be so few eligible men. Men are afraid of educated women and educated women are likely to be more selective of their prospective partner. The statistics seem to prove that a woman of thirty-five with a master's degree is more likely to be trampled to death by a herd of wombats in Pitt Street than to find a suitable male partner. But men are not really hiding in the bushes, only emerging at night to forage for food before returning to their hideouts before dawn. They are still around, of course, but their attitudes have changed during the last generation.

Women were not the only people liberated by the Pill: so were men. Regular sex did not necessarily have to lead to marriage: men and women could, as it were, have their cake and eat it too. And once one of the unspoken motivations for marriage had been removed, young men at the peak of their sexual drive could defer settling down while they lived a little. At the same time, many women in the feminist movement were questioning the value of marriage, saying it was institutionalised slavery, designed to keep men in positions of power, and that women shouldn't have a bar of it. Some men were also questioning marriage; not having women's biological urge to procreate, they saw marriage as a trap that benefited women more than men — as a life sentence of work and fidelity. What do they get out of marriage, they reason, that they can't have as single men? They can still find a woman to care for them. The very bad press that men have received in relation to marriage and divorce in the last twenty-five years has done little to convince them that marriage is a highly desirable proposition, either.

For the last twenty-five years, then, the entire rationale for marriage is being questioned. No longer do people take it for granted that marriage is the desired and desirable state for all adults. Men are choosing to stay single while others, having been married, left in disillusionment, deciding never to marry again. Men who do marry are tending to wait until their late twenties or early thirties. The women they are with may want to settle down and have children, and are therefore more likely to favour marriage, and they exert a good deal of pressure on the men to make a legal commitment. But now men are more wary, less convinced they will meet women's high expectations.

Men often have preconceived notions of what marriage means. Their expectations are based on early childhood conditioning, particularly the relationship with the mother. If that relationship was indulgent — he was special, his every need being met by an over involved and overprotective mother — then the man will approach adult relationships in the same way, expecting women to meet his needs before they met their own. If this indulgence bordered on smothering, a man is likely to react negatively to women trying to do things for him, and develop a strong need to be in control of the relationship. Maternal indifference would lead him to have a poor self-image and little expectation that his needs would be met by women. This means that he would probably be very well-defended from further hurt and tend to exploit the women in his life.

Childhood learning also influences a woman's approach to new friendships and sexual relationships with men, but her connection with her emotions and her closer emotional relationships with other people will make these less threatening for her than for him.

When we look at men and marriage, we really begin to see the negative consequences — for both men and women — of men's lack of awareness of their own emotional natures. His fear of vulnerability will tend to be greater than hers; when a man approaches a woman who is expecting a meaningful relationship, he is, from the outset, ill-prepared by his unequal competence in the areas of human emotions and intimacy.

Marital dissatisfaction is one of the least well-addressed problems in our society. For many men, their lack of fulfilment in the marriage is masked by their absorption in their jobs, as their absence from the home for most of the week tends to make their unhappiness more bearable. This unhappiness can and must be forgotten, or else the job may be in jeopardy. So the average man lives two lives: he is the mate at work who never lets on that anything is amiss at home, and the husband and father who resents the lack of fulfilment in his marriage but who doesn't know what to do about it.

> The expectation that I have the total responsibility for the economic health of the family really pisses me off.

> I'm in a very traditional marriage. I work six days a week and she looks after the kids and the home.

Despite the careers of their partners, most men will see themselves as responsible for the economic viability of their family: women see paid work as a choice for at least a part of their lives, but men see work as a lifetime's necessity. They expect that they will have children at some time, and that their wives will either temporarily or permanently give up their jobs to raise the children.

The impact of this knowledge on men is that they often see themselves as trapped, caught in a bind that shifts the relationship from one of love and free will to one of responsibility, duty and obligation for life (often relationships that have gone along happily while the couple were living together become problematical when they decide to marry). Many men who are unhappy with their work, who see themselves as unskilled or in the wrong career, find the thought of being unable to change because of the needs of the family to be a bleak prospect.

For men who are naturally ambitious, the family's material needs provide a rationale. It sounds better to say 'I'm working for the family' than to state 'I want power and status to help me like myself more.' So often they are accused of putting their job before the family and told, 'You're married to your job. If you paid as much attention to us as you do to your work, we'd all be much better off' and so on.

Some men find difficulty in seeing home and work as

separate, and are likely to say 'I'm doing this for the family. You all enjoy the benefits of my success.' Most men see their primary responsibilities as making certain that the family has a roof over its head, is well cared for and well educated. Any deficiency in providing these basic needs is likely to make men feel extremely guilty, and if accused he is likely to justify himself or even go on the attack 'What do you do with the money, then? Why don't you get a job?' and so on.

Sometimes the man sees the unwelcoming atmosphere of the home as a very poor return for all his efforts. Having been at work all day, he often looks forward to coming home. In fact, 'home' takes on the dimensions of an American situation comedy. Everybody will be happy to see him, dinner will be cooking, he and his wife will sit and chat, and he'll tell everybody what a rotten day he has had and they will all be sympathetic. Then, of course, reality hits: the kids are fighting, the place is a mess, his wife says 'You take over, I've had them. Let me tell you what they've done now.' When he asks what is for dinner, she says she hoped he'd go up the street and get some takeaway because she has had such a rotten day. He will shout at the kids because it's easier than picking on his wife, and he knows it's not her fault. But is this what married life is all about?

The fact that nearly 50 per cent of wives continue working after marriage has little bearing on man's general attitude to his responsibilities. Just as women have been biologically and socially prepared for the primary role of caregiver, so men have been prepared for their primary role as breadwinner. Each tends to glamorise and oversimplify the role of the other: men may say that their wives at home have it easy, they can decide how and when to complete the tasks of homemaking and mothering. Men often fail to acknowledge the negative side of homemaking, such as boredom, loneliness etc. Women may yearn to be free of the kids and out in the workforce, forgetting that much paid work is hard, mindlessly boring, or dirty — not to mention causing anxiety because of the added pressure to compete and succeed.

> I feel a sense of disappointment from my wife when I can't fix things around the house, but I'm hopeless at it. I never learned. I see her standing and drumming her fingers and saying 'What kind of man are you?' I know I only imagine this, but I put pressure on myself through my expectations of myself.

The strength of our expectations (not to say the biological conditioning) can be seen when we look at couples who have defied convention and reversed the traditional roles. They rarely sustain the change for more than a few years before reverting to the traditional patterns. It seems that the desire for change is often difficult to sustain in practice; the strong determinants of our marital roles, both biological and social, seem to have a magnetic pull. And besides, there is discrimination to consider. The house-husband will find it difficult to form the social connections his wife would take for granted: his sudden arrival at playgroup or his invitation to neighbouring wives to bring their children around to play will be seen in a very different light. A man's presence in an almost exclusively female domain will be as intrusive as that of a woman in a football team's dressing room; his very presence will change the nature of the group and, while this may be interesting at first, it will lead to his exclusion. Men and women speak gender-specific language, and a man has a view of himself that will make his fitting in almost impossible except on a one-to-one basis. His attempts to gain acceptance will be the same as those of any other outsider trying to gain entry: he will either try to impress by his value or try to gain support by his need. Both are well developed and universal joining rituals — but the problem is that they are both also mating rituals, likely to be recognised as such and to presuppose certain responses that in this context are inappropriate.

Marriage is the cornerstone of our society. The fact that choices can be made about whether or not we marry, and the 'rules' of the marriage, may make this important relationship easier, depending on the willingness of the partners to try and understand each other.

Ideally we should all be able to present ourselves to the world as we truly are, undefended, free of game-playing. But old defences are very important when encountering untested human beings for the first few times and, for many, these defences are never discarded — even in relationships that last a lifetime. The greater the potential for exposure, the more defensive the posture . . . and men are champions at defensive postures.

FATHERHOOD

> A lot of women seem to have an inbuilt desire to have a family. Children just appeared for me. I was quite ambivalent about them till they arrived. The last child, number four, was certainly not looked forward to by me — but when he came, it was a different story. I didn't feel keen for them (the children), but just let anyone try and take them away or hurt them!

> Women are driven to have babies, then most men catch up with the action.

When looking at the role of the father and his relationship with his children, it is important to accept that the reality of child-bearing will impose inevitable differences on the role of mother and father, which will tend to place the father at something of a disadvantage in terms of bonding with his children. No matter how eagerly a father anticipates the coming of his child, he cannot possibly feel the same way as does a woman who has carried a baby for nine months and experienced its growth, the changes in her hormones and her metabolism. The father's anticipation has no concrete reality apart from his partner's swelling belly, swollen feet and morning sickness.

The movement in the 1960s and 1970s to bring childbirth out of the arena of mysterious sickness and into the range of normal, natural processes was a great step forward for fathers. No longer were they to be seen as interfering in the exclusive province of doctors and midwives. The birthing process started to take place in settings more like normal bedrooms and less like morgues or torture chambers. Fathers were able to experience second-hand the process that their partners experienced in bringing forth their offspring.

If they were anything like me, they found the experience astounding. I will never forget the first time I saw a baby being born; it was our second child. My wife gave birth to her at home, in our own bed. It was the most moving experience of my life. Nothing I had imagined could have prepared me for this: the cries, the sweat, the stretch to breaking point of skin and nerves and muscle. I felt frightened out of my wits, helpless in the face of my wife's pain, yet feeling deep love for her because she was so strong. And then the baby came (how could such a large object possibly emerge from such a small opening?) and we smiled and cried.

Childbirth was no longer solely women's business: it was family business. Fathers were beginning to be persona grata at the birth of their children, instead of irksome nuisances patronised and ignored by hospital staff and made to feel guilty for their wives' pain and suffering. They experienced the bonding that a shared, momentous event produces. Some men had a chance to bond with their new-born children for the first time.

But wait . . . breastfeeding was back in fashion. One up for mothers and babies, one down for fathers. Those fathers who wanted a closer bonding with their children as babies were relegated to fetching and carrying, or changing nappies. Their role was very secondary. For many fathers, the time to have physical contact with the baby was after it had been fed, bathed and changed; the father might nurse it or play with it until it went to sleep or started to cry, at which point most fathers handed the baby to the mother. And why didn't the father attempt to pacify the baby himself? Well, if a close bond has developed between mother and baby from the outset, it is likely that the mother is more secure for the baby at times of stress. The more the mother succeeds in pacifying the baby, the more skilled she becomes at it: a self-fulfilling prophecy. At least bottle feeding gave men a better chance to bond if they chose to take their turns at feeding.

But the problem for fathers, too, is that they are not usually around when a lot of the action is taking place. They are likely to be at work when the baby is awake, and even if the baby wakes in the middle of the night demanding milk, women and song, men especially would much rather get some sleep.

The fact remains that, despite their best intentions, most fathers with young children have to work harder than their wives to develop a truly close relationship with them. Many fathers have direct contact with their children only at night or on weekends. The traditional divisions of labour do little to redress this imbalance. If men are the doers, the fixers, the outside workers, the weekends represent little change in the amount of contact between father and child. Painting, mowing, cleaning gutters or fixing the car are hardly suitable activities for babies and toddlers.

For the child, then, father is often seen as a special mysterious person, desirable, scary, different, unfamiliar:

when this important person plays with the child, it's no wonder there is constraint.

Dr Don Edgar, Director of the Institute of Family Studies, says in his paper 'The Role of the Father':

> Males comprise 71 per cent of all characters shown in all TV program types, 59 per cent of all characters in what could be called 'family role' programs, and 83 per cent of all those in non-fiction programs.

Yet when we compare this with reality, with what dads actually do in the home with and for their children, they are sadly missing. Contrary to the TV fantasy, children miss having a father who communicates, they wish he would stop working and start listening and caring, and they suffer a diminishing of self-esteem because this powerful figure seems to see them as unimportant.

The fact that almost half the adult potential for child development is being denied to children is not just a shame, it is a national disgrace. Men can no longer pretend they don't have time for children when women manage to find time for it as well as do work outside the home. Such a male copout must be exposed and the importance of male input to parenting reasserted.

> My father would never let us kids go out to play in case he thought of something for us to do.

Significantly, men are being challenged by men, rather than by women, to re-evaluate the part they play in rearing their own children. The aloof, distant, authoritarian Victorian father was replaced by a less strict but by and large equally unavailable father. But now men must come down from their self-constructed pedestals and play in the dirt with their kids. Men can no longer remain people their children may love but do not know. Not only do they need to play with their children but also carry out the day to day tasks of child-rearing: feeding, washing, cleaning-up — it is only through spending time on a daily basis with their children that men will be able to learn and to demonstrate the softer nurturing aspects of their personality.

This is particularly true for girls. While on superficial investigation boys would appear to fare better than girls — fathers are more likely to instruct sons than daughters — this is not true. Both girl and boy children experience their fathers as less available than their mothers in the early years, so both have to overcome distance to relate to their fathers. But if the father sees himself as having more responsibility for instructing his son, the boy is supposed to have most contact with the parent to whom he is less connected, in contrast to the girl, who spends more time with the bonded parent. The likely outcome is easy to observe. Gender stereotypes tend to be reinforced, producing girls more in touch with their feelings and more connected, and boys more instrumental and out of touch.

In a great many families, this issue of gender role rigidity has been tackled with enthusiasm by determined parents motivated to change this imbalance once and for all. They have non-sexist toys, boys are given dolls and girls have trucks; father changes nappies and cooks and cleans; mother attends car and house maintenance classes. Undoubtedly these changed attitudes have done much to address the issue of gender difference but the problem of the relationship between fathers and their children is still with us, despite these useful movements towards a greater equality. Whilst his son and daughter may feel less bound by the traditional expectations decreed by their biology and society, the father's connectedness is still less than that of his partner and it is this difference, rather than the absolutes, that makes the task hard for fathers. Many fathers feel that they never catch up, that what they do is never enough.

When I compare the fathers I see in my practice today with those I saw twenty years ago, they are quite different. The father of the 1990s has become substantially more involved emotionally with his family than he was a generation earlier, but growing with this change have been the expectations he places on himself and that society places on him.

These heightened expectations of the role of fathers and mothers seem to have developed from increasing focus on the needs of the child. Society has swung the pendulum from childhood being seen as an area unworthy of consideration and investigation to one where the child's needs seem to predominate over those of the adults. Perhaps we have Freud and his insights to thank for this change; as long as we believed that our genes, God or fate determined our future, there was little point in meddling. You just waited until the kids grew up and got on with their destinies, hoping in the meantime you could stop them from shaming you or dying.

This process of taking a fresh look at childhood probably received encouragement from the baby boomers. At one point Australia seemed awash with babies: there were baby health centres, antenatal classes, child psychologists, psychiatrists, mothercraft nurses — a whole industry depended on babies, not to mention the magazines, books, lectures, TV and radio and advice services. We were now focusing on more than babies' survival and physical well-being, we were interested in their emotional and psychological health. We wanted to know what they felt, thought and dreamed; these questions were important if we were to be good parents and help them develop their embryonic potential.

By the time this movement to recognise children as people in their own right had gathered enough momentum to be self-sustaining, it was becoming unstoppable. The focus on the needs of the child had blossomed into a preoccupation with children's needs to the exclusion of almost everything else, particularly the needs of the parents.

The needs of the children did, and for many parents still do, continue to dominate the household functioning. We run the risk of producing a generation of precocious children and exhausted parents. The social pressure to give our children at least as good if not better opportunities than their peers has led to a vicious circle of greater and greater effort on the part of parents to fulfil these expectations. We have the familiar spectacle of two parents with a child in each car racing off to ballet classes, physical culture classes, netball, soccer, parties, etc., every Saturday and Sunday, and on many week nights. It is hard to determine just who is driving this whole circus. It is clear that, for the most part, parents have very little time to relate as husband and wife or to spend time relating directly with their children. Many fathers feel frustrated by this endless cycle of taxiing and waiting, yet see themselves unable to change the process without being accused of selfishness or not caring about their children's happiness. A man's desire to spend more time with his wife, or just sit or potter, may raise guilt feelings in his partner about not being a good parent or a good homemaker; his apparent idleness is interpreted as a lack of care for the children and a devaluing of her and her role.

As the main responsibility for the comfort and warmth of the home tends to be carried by the woman, she is more likely to become aware of the needs around the house, just as the man is more likely to detect a whine in the differential or a knock in the motor of the car. When we feel responsible, we are sensitised to whatever may go wrong or need maintenance.

One persistent complaint men express in relation to their role as fathers is the sense of being controlled by their wives. A man is likely to say 'I feel that all the decision-making about what the kids do has been made before I get to hear about them. I just have to accept or object, no discussion.' Or 'I'm an outsider in the family. They seem to think I'm only useful for paying the bills and driving the car. I don't get asked any more, I get told. Oh it's always polite, but when the arrangements have already been made, what can you do? In the end, I just go along with it.' The persistence of this theme indicates that it has validity, and it bears further scrutiny.

The responsibility that women carry for the smooth running of the family places them in a bind. Whilst they see themselves as responsible, they are clearly unable to carry out all of the tasks themselves, either through lack of hours in the day, lack of skills or appearing to dominate the relationship and take control. No matter how the task is couched, an instruction is an instruction: 'Paint the gutters before they fall down', 'Do you think we could have someone in to paint the gutters?' 'If I dance naked on the top of the television, will you paint the gutters?' The packaging is different but the message is the same: 'Get your act together, Buster. If you don't care, why should I?'

The materialism of our urban existence makes this a never-ending cycle: replacement, repair, update, remodel, renew, rework, remove, relocate. It is not that a woman is unable or unwilling to do the work herself; she needs her role to be acknowledged. If she is judged and, more importantly, judges herself on her ability to provide a warm, comfortable setting for the family, her partner supports her ego when he also participates in these tasks. His insensitivity to her efforts in this area can and often does lead to major misunderstandings between men and women. He sees her asking him to help hang the curtains or buy a new lounge as nagging and putting pressure on him. She sees him as uncaring and self-indulgent. When he accuses her of trying to control his life, she is incredulous: What is he talking about? Doesn't he have all the power, don't I have to beg him to do things around the house? He is cast in the role of lord and master, she is the nagging, controlling wife.

The issues of what they both want from life, how they can spend more time together, what their long-term goals are, are rarely addressed. The man feels trapped in the rat race by his responsibility to his family and their expanding needs. The ability to deal with these very vital issues of lifestyle expectations requires a level of communication between the parents that is non-threatening, in which matters of sensitivity can be aired without either becoming defensive. This is a tall order for many couples, who go through life propelled by hidden forces they feel unable to locate, let alone control. Consequently issues of lifestyle are rarely addressed within the relationship.

Unfortunately, a great many fathers see little evidence of their value as people because their often long working hours plus travelling time mean that the children are either in bed or on their way there or doing homework when Dad arrives home. The gossip of the day has been heard, the issues discussed and resolved without his presence. This is hardly surprising, since in many instances the children have had hours with their mother before Dad arrives home. What often happens as a result of this distance is that fathers find it hard to relate easily to their children. The children see Dad as hard to approach and difficult to relax with and he sees his children as lacking warmth and love for him. He will often envy the easy way his children talk to their mother but feel unable to achieve the same easy, relaxed relationship.

He is out of reach of the children through his own behaviour, and the wife's protecting his relationship with them inadvertently exacerbates the alienation: 'Your father is tired, wait until he is in a better mood before you ask him.' Or, if the parents are at war: 'He's just a cranky old bastard, there's no point in asking him, he's never given anything away. Don't tell him, we'll work it out ourselves.'

This seemingly kindly behaviour by the mother is, by its very nature, alienating the relationship between father and children. The more he has an interpreter, the fewer skills children and father develop in relating effectively with one another. Father is seen in an unreal light by his children; the way they see him is not how he sees himself. He feels the need to live up to the expectations placed on him, to be a super Dad, heroic, successful, and wise, etc. Yet this need to be seen in a positive light by his children is all based on a false premise, leading only to distance and alienation. In order to have a relationship the participants need to be able to be themselves, warts and all. The need is for real people to relate in a real way.

The children's narrow perception of their father can encourage them to see him as irrelevant, lacking the capacity to meet their needs. In many households this view is aided and abetted by the father who is willing to be seen as a money-tree and little else, devaluing the time he could spend with his children, either through selfishness or lack of understanding. Some sports are very supportive of this kind of hands-off fathering, particularly those that are exclusively adult and take up most of the weekend.

The impact of this all-too-common emotional distance between fathers and their children is felt most severely by sons. They so often wind up suppressing the desire for emotional closeness with their father and converting that need into pseudo self-sufficiency. What emerges is typical male behaviour: toughness, imperviousness to hurt, decrying those of their peers who don't follow the lead. Boys who refuse to accept the status quo and still show their emotionality in public will be quickly labelled and become outsiders, thereby increasing their sense of loneliness and differentness. When toughness is the norm, sensitivity is doubly hard. If the reverse were true and emotional connectedness was the chosen style, at least those who didn't fit, the outsiders, could insulate themselves from the hurt by denying it. The present need for toughness leaves those who admit to their feelings as having to directly experience them through the pain of rejection and alienation. It is very hard to be an outsider.

> When I see my kids, I can see the echoes of me walking through the door.

The process of male alienation seems inexhaustible, passed on from generation to generation, with the need for closeness being mostly unmet. Many boys seem to be trapped in an endless cycle of emotional hunger.

The need for emotional closeness is universal. We are all born with that inbuilt drive and it is essential for our early survival. To be held and fed, changed and rocked provides the two-way connection that will later become the sophisticated behaviours of our adult caring, loving and sexuality. The infant knows that this need must be met and will develop a variety of techniques for having them met. Crying, smiling, snuggling, reaching out to be picked up, all these gestures will trigger a reciprocal response in the parent. Stimulus/response, the transaction completed. What then happens if the child starts to get the message that the needs are inappropriate? That it was all right to be picked up and snuggled last year, but it isn't now? That once I could cry when I was frightened but now I have to be a big boy like Daddy? The words don't have to be spoken; the modelling is taking place every waking hour. If I want to grow up to be a man like Daddy then I must give up these needs and pretend that I'm brave when I'm terrified, that I'm strong when I'm weak, that I'm clever and know things that I don't. That's what men are and do.

The whole issue of the role of the father must include an assessment of what men think women want of them as fathers, as the basic ingredient in a loving relationship is the desire to please the other in order to get rewarded. It is therefore important to have a clear picture of the partner's expectations if the effort is going to bear fruit. And one of the problems for fathers lies in the fact that many women are uncertain and give confusing or contradictory messages.

Like most of the relationships between men and women, parenting is undergoing great upheaval. The drive for self-definition and self-expression is often projected onto the children; it becomes the parents' desire to make certain that their children's lives have more meaning, that they are more fulfilled, than their parents. For many parents, the goals of personal self-expression and providing the best opportunities for their children are in conflict. The attainment of one leads to the loss of the other, and both parents feel the dilemma. Fathers often see themselves being expected to provide the income for the children's self-development, whether through private schooling, coaching, toys, clothes or outings, yet at the same time feel they are expected to be closer to their children, to take a greater interest in their activities, talk to them, etc. The duality of these requests is often seen as contradictory by the father who, like the mother, sees his own needs being unmet and his need to earn an income preventing him from spending time with his children, even if he knew how to enjoy their company.

No wonder men are often seen as insensitive to their family's emotional needs after the children have left babyhood. The contradiction of having to be a warrior at work and an empathic father at home often leaves our hapless father reeling. The business world is dominated by men who have resolved their roles of husband, father, boss by becoming money trees, convincing themselves that providing wealth for their families more than compensates for their physical and emotional absence. In this climate of self-justification it is hardly surprising that the man who says he can't stay back for a meeting after work because he has to pick up the children will be labelled as lacking in ambition and not having the organisation's interests at heart — not a good candidate for promotion. This process of self-selection by values will ensure that the change that would help men reassess their personal value to their children will be a long time coming.

Fathering has changed substantially in the past fifty years and many factors that underpinned the role in the past no longer exist. The society into which our fathers and grandfathers were born was substantially more orderly and structured than ours. The lowly status of women provided a convenient back for men to stand on, and the even lower status of children created a useful human pyramid, with father standing at the apex. We have seen how unstable this foundation was, yet at the time fathers went on with their fathering tasks unaware of the danger to their authority that was to come. My father held a deep conviction in the rightness of his position. His views were dogmatic and unshakeable. His pronouncements were expected to be accepted without question and none of us were allowed to challenge his authority. This certainty of the father's authority was widely supported in the community both by its institutions, the church, the schools, the business community, as well as by the population at large. His home was his castle and anything, short of murder, that took place under his roof was his business. He was truly king of his castle.

This divine right that fathers enjoyed was something of a double-edged sword. The self-certainty it produced provided a strong sense of consistency and security in the family, in the time-honoured tradition of true leaders.

The negative side of this position was in the potential to abuse that power, either through misguided direction or malice. The men also missed out on the ability to opt out and give the role to others. Most of the problems with nineteenth-century fathering was not in the father's relationship with his children — that was merely a symptom. It was in his relationship with his wife. The hierarchy both elevated him above and out of reach and relegated her to a role that could only exercise power covertly. He lost the potential of joint leadership that could leaven the excesses of both mother and father and provide support for one another in the care and control of the children. What he had instead was often palace intrigue.

The progressive collapse of the power structure that previously upheld the role of father has clearly brought enormous benefits not only to women and children but also to men. The rewards are easy to see. Perhaps we also need to look at the other side. Rarely does change bring only benefits, despite the lengths to which the proponents of change will go to in trying to convince us otherwise. It is usually not until the change has reached the point of irreversibility that we start to see the true cost. Nuclear power was to free mankind, wars were to bring lasting peace, economic development would bring freedom from poverty, Aboriginal assimilation would solve all of their problems — the list is endless.

So it has been with the decline in absolute authority of fathers. It has been replaced by uncertainty and tentativeness by many men who, dissatisfied with the fathering they experienced themselves and aware of the isolation of authoritarianism, have sought an alternative relationship. Those who fail to discriminate between clear and consistent leadership and authoritarianism, however, find themselves outmanoeuvred by their children. They have retreated to a position that is unhelpful to their children. Instead of being a source of strength and guidance, fathers try to be their children's friend. Indulgence is the reverse side of the parenting coin to authoritarianism. With authoritarianism, the child fails to adequately develop self-confidence in decision making, seeking approval from others who appear strong and decisive. Indulgence, on the other hand, leaves the child with inadequate self-control and direction; he or she will carry quite unrealistic expectations of others meeting their needs.

In order to be fulfilling for himself and his family, the father's role needs to be established on the firm foundation of an equal coalition with the role of the mother. Joint parenting provides the strength that the children need in order to feel emotionally safe to grow. Dual leadership provides the flexible strength that is the hallmark of effective parenting, just like the laminated samurai sword that is legendary for its strength because it consists of layers of steel banded together. Those early sword makers realised that there was no point in making blades harder as they were brittle and broke under stress; what they needed was strong flexibility. In order for the weapon to be effective the bond between the layers had to be inseparable. The whole is greater than the sum of the parts.

Parents working in unison don't need to be hard to be strong. Both can be soft and strong as the circumstances demand without having to pretend to be something they are not in order to parent effectively. The love that parents feel for their children can be given direct rather than indirect expression and so we can do away with the notion that the roles are divided into the soft and hard 'you just wait till your father comes home' style of parenting.

HAVING AFFAIRS

> I like to flirt. It boosts my ego. But once she takes it seriously, I'm caught in a bind. It's like when you chase something, never expecting to catch it. And when you do, what do you do with it?

All long-term relationships, including marriage, are vulnerable to a third party (either male or female) simply because, over time, people tend to become not only familiar with each other but also bored. We all have a limited repertoire of behaviours and responses, so idiosyncrasies that seem amusing on the first encounter and possibly thereafter, can be irritating ten years on. Additionally, eye-catching, impressive and flirtatious behaviour cannot be sustained; it is essentially short-lived in performance. Over time, mating rituals may be used on others rather than a partner who is already captive and unimpressed.

When I reflect on my counselling experience over the last twenty-plus years, I cannot detect a significant difference between the number of wives and husbands admitting to extramarital relationships. I am left with the distinct view that, while at times their motivation may be different, the end result is much the same. Perhaps one of the reasons why society sees men as more responsible for extramarital affairs is that they may feel more inclined to admit to their infidelities.

Because men have been taught competition rather than cooperation from an early age, by the time they reach manhood they have developed considerable skills in testing out the strengths and weaknesses of new acquaintances, whether male or female. Watch the verbal sparring men engage in when they're in new social situations, for instance. Few men would be aware that their methods of initiating social relationships are essentially defensive, designed to reduce their emotional vulnerability. They frequently dominate dinner-table conversation to the exclusion of all other participants, preening their intellectual feathers and watching the reactions of the spectators to detect admiration.

We all tend to retain behaviour patterns that work for us, and if a particular woman laughs at a man's joke while his partner groans, having heard it ten times before, he perceives the appreciating audience liking and understanding him, while his companion is putting him down.

Because men's preoccupation with sex is different from that of women, there is, at least on first encounter, a sexual tension partly increased by the man's estimate of the desirability, availability and response of the woman to him as a man. While part of this process will be below the level of awareness and will emerge only if the woman seems receptive to his friendliness, his behaviour will be part of a well-established and, to him, natural process of determining the future nature of the relationship.

However, men are often hooked inadvertently on their own bait and are surprised to find themselves with a mermaid on the end of the line when they were only showing-off, fishing for applause.

While some men are very well aware of the sexual games they play, many are relatively unaware of the impact their performance may have on women. If they are insensitive to their own and other people's emotions, they may fail to appreciate the nuances of sexual encounters. (This is where men really can't understand the way women work . . . while a man may be blissfully unaware of the network of emotions that connect people, a woman will be able to work out very rapidly who fancies whom. My own wife can tell me, from a voice tone on the telephone or body language at the door, those female clients who have formed a positive attachment to me and have started to perceive her as a threat. I marvel in disbelief at this facility — but experience has shown me her reliability!)

Because men and women tend to work from different frames of reference, men often seek out women to be their friends rather than other men. Men need understanding and acceptance of their insecurities and vulnerabilities, and they may not find this with other men — with whom, after all, they have been taught to compete. Besides, they may not expect other men to understand them; they need a guide to the world of emotions, which excludes other men as suitable candidates, for it would be the blind leading the blind.

The men I have worked with in groups all talked of being more likely to reveal themselves to women than to other men, but also of being uncertain of what women value in their friendship. Having little experience of true friendships, they tend to believe that being with, talking together, sharing emotions is insufficient in itself to sustain a friendship. Being doers by training, they will devalue being, seeing it as incidental to a friendship, rather than central to it. But they all say they are looking for understanding from a woman.

If a man does not find this acceptance and understanding at home, he will seek it outside. But what is the difference between an intimate friend and a lover? How are the distinctions drawn?

Men have great confusion in this area of their lives, being essentially unskilled in dealing with their own and other people's emotions. A woman developing a new relationship with a man needs to be aware that he will be struggling with the dual issues of 'What do I want from her?' but also 'What does she want from me, and how can I determine this?'

This may sound a strange cause for conflict to women who see themselves as being clear and unambiguous, but it is here that the failure to understand that men and women don't speak the same language will lead to continual confusion. She may be looking for sex, while he needs a soulmate, or vice versa. As men carry the responsibility for initiating sexual moves, a man will test out her desire for sex directly at some time, even if he only wants a friendship with a woman. He will do this in order to be on the safe side and not to be holding back when what she wants is his sexuality rather than his friendship.

Many men have become convinced that the Pill and the consequent sexual revolution have liberated women from the link between their hearts and their genitals — that they are now, like men, able to see sex as a sport, to distance themselves emotionally from their sexual behaviour. A man who has a one-night stand, for instance, is likely to be surprised and annoyed by a woman who implies that she was doing him a favour, that he owes her something in return, something more than their mutual enjoyment.

A man's view is likely to be: 'Before contraception was reliable and safe, women were undoubtedly taking great risks in having sex, but what's the big deal now? If women want sexual equality, they shouldn't complain if men see it as a pleasant episode rather than a prelude to something else.'

Like women, men have read the books and the magazine articles about women claiming the right to be sexual beings and, as a consequence, they may believe that women are just like themselves. There are strong grounds for believing that women have been trapped by their own publicity. It's a little like women confessing to rape fantasies and men believing this means they want to be raped. Men have failed to differentiate between the political and social needs for women to reclaim their sexuality, and their biological and emotional make-up — and there is strong evidence that women have themselves failed to make this distinction, too. Are they in fact kidding themselves that they are like men, that they can emotionally detach themselves from the sexual act?

Of course, both men and women may be driven by a desire for new sexual experiences. However, both need to consider what else is being sought in these relationships. As long as we see all men driven by the desire for sexual conquest, we will fail to look further than their genitals for explanations of their female friendships.

Of course, it is important to acknowledge that there are also significant numbers of bedroom commandos, who see women purely as sex objects to be chased and caught as quickly and efficiently as possible. As Tony, the young Cockney jockey in the brilliant BBC series *Seven Up*, which examines a group of people from all walks of life at seven-year intervals, says: 'The four Fs: find 'em, feed 'em, fuck 'em and forget 'em.' It is reassuring to report that, like most men, Tony outgrew this male bravado in the face of real relationships with women; he was last seen as a happily married man with a young family.

But some men don't change, and there is little doubt that those who fail to outgrow this macho posturing not only hold women in low regard but at a deeper level actually despise them — seeing each new conquest as another scalp for the belt, another notch on the weapon, another way of getting back at an unloving or rejecting mother. It's almost as though by screwing a woman they are literally laying the ghosts of past hurts. The problem with these men is that the reason for their exploitative use of women is never addressed; their anger and resentment rarely surface, and when they do they are likely to exacerbate rather than resolve the underlying problem. I can hear women saying: 'That's right, blame the mothers if men act badly towards women, that's just stopping men from being responsible for their own bad behaviour.' I see a difference between understanding cause and effect and condoning bad behaviour. Just as I can accept that a violent household will predispose children to violence as adults, either as victimisers or victims, I can understand the behaviour without in any way condoning the violence.

We cannot discuss men and affairs without considering the older man/younger woman phenomenon that is so common in our society. It is not unusual to see men with partners twenty to thirty years their junior, getting a new lease of life.

For every man of fifty who wants to prove himself to himself, there is a twenty-five-year-old willing to help him. Many of these men look very attractive to younger women; they tend to compare quite well to the woman's male partners in her own age group. Many of the men her own age will tend to be immature by comparison, still to establish themselves, with little disposable income, perhaps still more interested in going out with their male friends than in having an exclusive relationship with a woman. The older man is more likely to appreciate her attention than her younger boyfriends; an older man will see himself lucky to have her interested in him while a younger man may not think this is particularly special.

The tragedy in the older man/younger woman situation is the effect it may have on an existing marriage. To put it in economic terms, the twenty-five-year-old woman is enjoying the resources accumulated by two people over the years: not just the economic but the social and emotional resources. These have been developed in the breeding ground of wife and family, so it is not surprising that so many wives feel angry and bitter; after struggling through the hardest years of child rearing, going without, working together for what the woman perceived as common goals, someone else is making off with her investment. One of my clients said, when asked if she felt any concern for a discarded younger girlfriend of her husband, 'Why should I? She went into it with her legs wide open.'

In these situations the label of 'bastard' is usually pinned to the man without hesitation, by other men as well as by women. But it is important to remember that not all marriages are made in heaven. A male client said, as he sat and cried in my office, 'My wife's never been anything but bitter and angry. I can't live the rest of my life with a woman totally devoid of charity and compassion. I promised myself that I'd wait until the kids left home, and now they have and so will I.' It would be easy to see the motivation for this man's desire for a new partner as being merely sexual, but he was in fact seeking warmth and compassion.

Men will probably have different approaches to women depending on whether they are looking for sex or for a mate. They are basically conservative in their attitudes to women and, despite all the changes over the past twenty-five years, they still expect the women they marry to be less worldly than themselves — though the biological and emotional reality is different. Apart from that, they are likely to think that women are pretty much the same as they are. The consequence of this denial of gender differences is continued misunderstanding between men and women, with men seen as insensitive and exploitative and women considered manipulative.

SEPARATION AND DIVORCE

> I would have willingly set fire to all that we owned in fifty-dollar bills if I could have stayed married to my wife, and I'm the kind of person who looks down the menu to find the cheapest meal.

The relationship between men and women is often best and most accurately observed at major focal points in their lives: falling in love; getting married; having children; divorcing; getting sick; dying. These key periods give us a chance to see individuals stretched beyond their normal everyday existence. Under these circumstances a person's values, capabilities and capacities are put to the test — so those things we consider part of ourselves, part of our sense of self-definition, will either be confirmed or denied by our behaviour.

The decision to separate is one of these key points. In fact, there are three kinds of separation: the mandatory twelve months prior to divorce, the perpetual separation of couples whose marriage has ended but who, for religious or other reasons, will not divorce, and the 'fear of hurting' separation. Of the three, the third is probably the most difficult to deal with.

Many couples, though separated, are unwilling to admit to each other that the marriage has ended. Fearing the negative effect of the decision on their partner, not wanting to hurt him or her, they fudge the decision. Often they can admit the truth during marriage counselling, to say that the separation is really preparation for divorce. But unfortunately some couples drag the separation process on for years and years. The problem for the partner who has been left is that he or she is unable to grieve or get on with life. The state of suspension this entails often leads to the conclusion that if they only try harder, the marriage will be saved. The failure of the 'fear of hurting' partner — usually the one who has walked out on the relationship — to tell the truth, while expressing a desire to be considerate, is in fact very cruel. One of the inevitable consequences of the end of a relationship is loss of confidence, and this type of delayed announcement can have an absolutely devastating effect on the well-being of the partner who is being left.

In the twenty-plus years I have been counselling couples, a substantial change has taken place not only in the problems that couples present for resolution but in the balance of power in the relationship. Twenty years ago, about 75 per cent of the requests for counselling came from women, whose husbands were unwilling to attend, often seeing the problems as residing in the wife rather than in the relationship. Now, about as many requests for counselling come from men as from women, and the willingness of men to attend, even when they have not been part of the initial contact, has increased substantially.

But even more striking has been the change in the percentage of women wishing to leave the marriage, compared to men. A decade ago, the most common scene was a wife pleading with her husband not to leave. But now the picture has reversed and it is more likely to be the man who is begging his wife to stay and to give him another chance.

A man will say to his wife 'Look, why won't you let me prove to you that I can be different?' He will interpret his wife's dissatisfaction as being due to practical things that he can fix by using his familiar problem-solving skills.

Many men find underlying causes of women's discontent incomprehensible. A common question is 'Why do you want to leave me? What have I done wrong?' Or, if he perceives he has done something wrong (for example, had an affair) he will plead for forgiveness and another chance.

The truth is that many men have great difficulty in catching-up with the action in the marriage. Lacking the resources to monitor the emotional climate of the relationship, a man relies on his wife's reports to determine its relative health and, depending upon the seriousness of the report, will take action. The problem with this style of management is that too often it fails to address the underlying problems; it is largely management by damage control and appeasement. It's like the song about the hole in the roof — no need to fix it when the weather is dry, and you can't when it's raining.

Let's take a typical husband–wife interaction. For once, the husband gets a very clear message from the wife that she is unhappy. The message has undoubtedly been given before, but this time it exceeds his threshold of hearing. She is fed up with being taken for granted: he rarely takes her out, and when he does he ignores her and talks only to other people. Something always crops up to prevent their taking a holiday. She expresses all this, and he comes home early with flowers for a week, and arranges a nice dinner *à deux* at a restaurant (even though she has to make the bookings and arrange a baby sitter and he is late coming home). He is apologetic, they go out and enjoy the evening, come home and make love. The husband feels that, having understood the problem and done something about it, things will be fine from now on. He thinks his wife is happy now.

But in no time things revert to normal. She feels neglected and used; he will never understand her needs, she could spend the rest of her life shouting and nagging and getting the occasional sop, the occasional bone to keep her quiet. She wants more than this. Eventually she calls a halt to this self-defeating cycle of frustration, and he is absolutely bewildered.

He also feels abandoned, misused, betrayed and misunderstood. She is heartless and unsympathetic — hasn't he always been a good provider and a good husband? Hasn't he always listened when she complained? She seemed pretty happy most of the time, and when she said she wasn't, well, he did something to change things. So what was her problem?

Placed in this position, many men will justify themselves, and an easy way to do this is to compare their behaviour with that of other men. 'I don't go to the club after work, I don't play around, I don't see what you have to complain about.' Attack, of course, is the other form of defence: 'Look at you, you're so cold, when was the last time you approached me for sex? Why do I always have to make the first moves?'

The subtlety and fine nuances of behaviour are mostly lost on men, with only the overwhelming emotions being registered. Consequently, men lack the early warning system that most women take for granted. So men are frequently well behind the game when it comes to knowing the degree of emotional pain each is experiencing. As a result, when the distress falls below his threshold of awareness, it is gone, whilst at the same time his partner is probably still well within her discomfort zone, and wondering why he has forgotten the crisis and is carrying on as before.

As long as men lack the ability to easily monitor their own or their partner's emotional state, they will carry a fundamental flaw in their capacity to effectively run a relationship. As they are not able to label their own subjective state, men fly blind most of the time. When asked to express a feeling, they will describe a thought. In answer to the question 'How do you feel?' most men will preface their answer with 'I think' and then go on to express ideas or events. If the question is posed again and they are asked to refrain from the 'I think' preface, most men will say 'I don't know; okay, I suppose.' Even though our language contains a very rich lexicon of words to describe emotions, many men would be hard pressed to describe ten, never mind being able to match what is going on inside them with an accurate word.

> I don't see any point in going to work any more. I've worked twenty years for my family, house and garden. I'd give anything to be in my back garden mowing the lawn and watching the kids play. But what's the use, now I have to stand at the gate every second Saturday till the kids come out. I'm not even offered a glass of water.

The emotional disparity between men and women significantly disadvantages men if they are forced to deal with divorce from an emotional standpoint. The philosophy of 'If I can't see it, explain it or analyse it, it doesn't exist' serves men very poorly when it comes to dealing with loss and grief. The emotions that are likely to be generated by such a traumatic event as divorce will not be ignored. The body insists on their being taken seriously; physical problems, even breakdown, can result from denial of strong emotion. Sadness, pain, anger, guilt, self-doubt, remorse and many other feelings are integral to significant loss, and divorce is certainly that. Even if the marriage is admittedly over, and the couple have apparently little positive regard for each other, the grieving is as much about the loss of hope and a shared dream as it is about the loss of a partner.

> I know it had to end, but where do I go from here? My whole life has been based on being a husband and father, now what? What's the bloody point to it? I feel like chucking it all in.

If we accept that a large part of a man's self-esteem is based on his role, then the loss of that role through divorce — the loss of his family home and regular contact with his children and his wife — can lead him to question the purpose of his life. Under these circumstances, just about every man feels like a failure. The way men see things, a real bloke raises a family and provides for them and anyone who doesn't succeed in that role has messed things up. While a man may publicly express relief or bravado about the separation or divorce, privately he feels he is less of a man.

It is a fact that men are more than twice as likely to suicide post divorce than women. A recent review in Western Australia reveals a dramatic change in the rate of attempted suicide between 1972 and 1987: female rates fell 9 per cent, while male rates rose *47 per cent*. The age groups experiencing the most dramatic rise were fifteen to nineteen years and forty to forty-four years. Both age groups also represent times when men are either starting relationships, or are in the most divorce-prone periods in their marriage. They also represent peak periods in men's employment prospects. The first time is a particularly stressful one for young males, who see themselves in our patriarchal society as needing the career that will support a family for an entire working life. The second is the age group where the midlife crisis is most common, the details of which are well documented elsewhere.

The idea that men are able to effectively conduct their

own lives and lead other people's, is clearly flawed. They are vulnerable to the same vagaries of life as are women, yet they have fewer resources to combat them. If a man's mother dies, ten to one his wife will help him deal with the loss, give him permission to cry, make space for his grieving and, perhaps through her own sadness, provide a model for his own behaviour. When a man is alone, he is much more likely to repress his feelings and cover his grief with activity, to try not to think, not to feel.

Some men will try and prove to themselves and the world that they are okay by running around, trying to sleep with any women who will have them. Feeling they have nothing to lose, they will embark on what they would have previously considered irresponsible behaviour. Now is the time to fulfil their fantasies, why not? But, as many women will agree, this is often self-defeating, for their bravado isn't matched by their performance, and the result is an even greater sense of failure. And, given the choice, most men would prefer security and reinstatement to the family home over one-night stands and an empty home unit.

The popular view of the free-spending, bed-hopping divorced or separated man living the high life is about as unreal as the image of the gay divorcee. The reality is more likely to be loneliness, empty week nights and weekends spent alone going to the movies, eating alone, trying to work up enthusiasm for meeting people but lacking the energy or desire. The truth is that when people have been married for ten or fifteen or twenty years, they have lost the skills that are the stock-in-trade of the singles. Many people who married young have never developed the capacity to meet strangers, to strike up a conversation, to ask someone out for a date. They feel completely out of their depth in the settings in which the singles suss out the market.

We've discussed some of the reasons why men seem to take the loss of a relationship harder than women.

There are other compelling reasons that also need to be addressed.

As the mother becomes the custodial parent in more than 90 per cent of cases, the most common outcome of divorce for men is the loss of regular contact with their children and the loss of the family home. While the wife's life will undoubtedly change for the worse economically (single-parent households are the largest group below the poverty line), she at least is much more likely to retain close contact with her children and also the familiar surroundings of home, friends and family possessions.

Many women wanting to end the marriage will try to encourage their husbands to leave the house by fair means or foul. Should she have sought legal advice, the idea of getting him to leave rather than leaving herself will be reinforced very strongly, in order not to prejudice her case for custody should the matter go to court.

> She could have the lot, I only took my clothes. I hadn't worked all that time to build a home only to tear it down. Just because the marriage was over didn't mean we had to squabble over the spoils.

I have often worked long and hard with separating couples and reached agreements that met the needs of the husband, the wife and the children, only to have all my work suddenly go up in smoke after the intervention of an overenthusiastic lawyer, who has convinced one of the parties that he or she is being disadvantaged.

Many lawyers I know agree that the place for settling custody disputes is outside the court system in the hands of trained mediators, with the decision being taken back to the court for ratification. A courtroom is hardly the ideal setting for making decisions that affect the long-term future of innocent children. The law is cumbersome at the best of times, so its capacity to deal effectively with such delicate matters as family dynamics is almost non-existent. It usually creates more problems than it resolves in such matters as custody and property disputes. In the last analysis, the family must find a way of working together if the parents are going to fulfil the expectations of jointly raising their offspring.

Divorce behaviour is a very informative area to study for understanding male attitudes towards women, wives, men and children. Because the media tend to report only conflict and disaster, the behaviour of those couples who successfully negotiate the minefield of divorce tends to be unreported. So images of children being abducted by disgruntled parents, endless custody battles, the nauseating spectacle of the wealthy fighting over millions of dollars' worth of property and investments tend to dominate public perception of divorcing behaviour. It is little wonder that there is a widely-held belief that people at the end of a marriage are likely to behave towards each other in ways that deny the existence of any mutual caring or regard. This inaccurate view needs to be addressed.

However, the process of dispossession is usually more painful for men than is generally understood. For the man who leaves, the prospects, unless he is wealthy, are rather bleak.

The average man will probably live in a bedsit or a one-bedroom unit to begin with, with few friends and scant furnishings: how can you divide a household established for a family into two? Half a fridge, half a washing machine, dryer, dinner set, double bed, lounge suite, garden tools, dog? Chances are, if the children are staying with their mother, the father will take only the bare essentials; the bits of crockery that don't match, the old cutlery that is never used. For some men, this prospect of picking over the family's possessions is too hurtful and distasteful, so they literally leave with their clothes and little else. This is not to imply that men are more altruistic, less likely to want the family assets split down the middle, but relates to the sense of belonging and comfort derived from being surrounded by familiar things and people.

The reality of men's dispossession following separation leads to further complications for their mental health. At the time of separation, there is often a modicum of goodwill between the couple, so that wives will offer their husbands unlimited access to the children. A typical comment is 'I know you love them and the kids need their father, so I won't stand in the way of your being with them.' Over time, this generosity will dissipate in the face of reality. It is often painful for a former wife to be constantly in the presence of her former husband, so 'Why don't you stop for dinner when you bring them home' becomes 'I won't be home when you come, so leave them with the neighbours.'

This change of heart may also reflect the children's dissatisfaction with the arrangements. Children and parents relate to one another within a context; change that context and connectedness becomes difficult. The interaction between parents and children is mostly about daily activities: 'What was school like today?', 'What will you have for breakfast?', 'Do you still have a tummy ache?' Deep and meaningful discussions occur once in a blue moon. The routine of their daily lives gives both parent and child grounds for relating. The parent who has little access to this ordinary world of school, home and friends is seriously disadvantaged. Conversation becomes stilted, all the toys are at home with the bikes, games and friends. Their father doesn't remember what foods they like and dislike. He doesn't have anywhere the kids can play (the unit has no garden) so they go out, eat fast food, go to the movies, the park. Any observant person can see the non-custodial parents at the weekends wandering around the shops and parks with bored kids, killing time until they have to be taken back home again, the fathers wondering why they are bothering when the kids seem to get so little out of it. The artificiality of trying to be a parent in public and trying to entertain children who would normally be entertaining themselves at home frequently leads to breakdown in the relationship between the father and his children.He may see them as uninterested in him, only coming over to see him for what they can get, always asking for money to be spent on them: 'They have become mercenary since I left. She's probably putting them up to it so that she doesn't have to spend anything herself. With all the maintenance I've got to pay her, I've barely enough left to live on, never mind indulging the kids.'

Few men can overcome the obstacles to a close and continuing relationship with their children after a divorce. Those fathers who do, despite the difficulties, are to be congratulated for their perseverance — they are rewarding both themselves and their children. I always encourage non-custodial parents to persevere with the relationship, whatever the children or their custodial parent state as the children's needs. If the children don't want to visit, phone regularly; if they aren't allowed to answer the phone, write to them; remember the important days in their lives, keep in contact through the school, go to sports days, speech nights. It is too late when told by a grownup child 'I didn't think you loved me, you didn't seem to be interested in me.' If nothing else, one message needs to register with the child: 'I love you and I'll always love you. Even if I can't be with you, I'll always be here for you if you need me.'

It is a sad fact that five years after divorce, more than half of the non-custodial fathers have lost regular contact with their children. This is an enormous tragedy as all the family miss out. Some men feel particularly bitter about having to financially support children with whom they have no contact, particularly when the loss of contact is not of their making, for example, when the family move from the district or when access is legally permitted but functionally denied. Whereas the law clearly states that access is a right of the child, not the parent, many custodial parents use access as a weapon pointed at the head of the former spouse in order to ensure their compliance: 'If you don't . . . the children won't come for Christmas.'

Much of the misunderstanding generated between former husbands and wives is quite unintentional, existing largely because they don't talk to each other. The onus of responsibility for keeping the father informed of what goes on in the lives of the children clearly lies with the custodial mother. Often the failure to inform is an oversight rather than a deliberate desire to withhold, but the person frozen out is hardly likely to see it in that light. To him it's deliberate, a way of influencing the kids against him. Paranoia is much more likely when there is an information vacuum; the absence of facts leads to speculation and when that speculation is about a former partner who has hurt you then it is probably going to be negative.

As many men have been emotionally and physically peripheral to their children, even when they all lived under the same roof, they will be doubly disadvantaged when trying to build a good relationship at a distance. It is obvious that many a father becomes overwhelmed by the task and withdraws altogether, believing that the behaviour of the children towards him indicates that they don't need him and don't love him. Unable to differentiate between his children's rejecting and distant behaviour and their need and love for him, he sets up a self-fulfilling prophecy: 'My kids don't like me, I'll disappear, they never ring or write, I was right.'

While many fathers love their children but stay away through feelings of rejection, many fathers desert their children without an apparent second thought. But our society frequently fails to differentiate between the abandoning fathers and the substantial group who become disillusioned by their lack of meaningful contact with their children and give up.

What happens to all those people who end their first marriage in the divorce courts? The vast majority remarry; after five or more years, more than three-quarters will be in new relationships, either remarried or living together on a permanent basis. The non-custodial parent (read male) will certainly be much better placed than his former wife to make a new relationship. His ease of movement and freedom from the daily responsibility of children, his higher earning capacity and his ease of contact with people through his work all give him a distinct advantage. In addition the older man younger woman habit will ensure that the range of available partners is considerably larger for divorced men than for divorced women.

Men who choose younger partners cop a good deal of flak, particularly from other women. It is almost as if they have been cheating, breaking the rules that say: stick with your own age group; what about all those women your own age who are very eligible and wanting a partner? In my experience, the twenty-five to thirty-five-year-old single woman knows exactly what she is doing and is as much in charge of this part of her life as any other. Many women in this age group have started to despair of the possibility of the men in their own age range ever being prepared to commit themselves to a long-term relationship. (One of the stories doing the rounds illustrates the case: 'What does a single woman do to get rid of cockroaches? She asks them to make a commitment.')

A person leaving an unhappy marriage is extremely vulnerable to the offer of tenderness and warmth from anyone who will make the offer. The emotional barrenness which characterises most failing marriages predisposes the participants to respond positively to another's tenderness and care. Men's lack of skills in forming intimate relationships with other men means that they lack friendships that will support them in their grieving: a man either does it alone or finds a woman who will listen.

As a consequence, too many divorced men move into new relationships long before they are ready. Women can find themselves in love with someone who spends more time talking about his former wife than about her, spending what she thought would be romantic trysts dealing with his anger or hurt over past events and feeling that she has become more familiar with his former wife than with her own best friend. In those circumstances the relationship can be doomed before it ever rises off the ground, partly because both parties carry very different expectations that are never understood. His primary need is for someone to help him through his pain, someone sympathetic and understanding who will provide some of the comforts, like sex and a place to belong, that are now missing from his life. The problem is that vulnerable men can be quite attractive, being more open and less wary than usual, so a woman can easily believe that she has found the real thing: here is a man who is sensitive and self-aware, in touch with his feelings, prepared to let his defences down. Here is the kind of man to have children with, not the usual jock whose most profound expression of sensitivity is 'Shit, that was great!', whose self-expression consists of a series of grunts and moans, or who runs for cover at the first sign of strong emotion either positive or negative. How is she to know that it is probaby all transient and that when he has had enough tender loving care he will probably put his armour back on and roll up his tent and go back to being a 'real man'?

We all tend to delude ourselves by choosing to see those things we want to see and ignoring the contrary, and this is certainly true in mate selection. If love is not totally blind, it is at least very short-sighted and the correcting spectacles it uses are mostly rose-coloured. Little wonder that second marriages entered into during this grieving process stand a high risk of going the same way as the first one.

REMARRIAGE

> I always feel a sense of disloyalty to my own children when I take my stepchildren out and we have a good time. I know it is illogical because my own children live interstate, but I often wonder who is giving them a good time.

Men who marry women much younger than themselves will often feel an initial sense of pride in being able to succeed where younger men have failed, their ego getting a boost from the knowledge that other men may envy them. In the competitive male world, he can be a symbol of success. The problem with winning a young heart is that you have to keep it. Like the old bull seal who is only as good as his next fight, the older man can have anxious moments wondering if he'll still be desirable in ten or twenty years.

The problem is exacerbated if he has teenage sons who may well be closer in age to his new wife than he is himself. This can easily lead to unreasonable jealousy that is never expressed directly but comes out in other ways. He may decide that it's time the boys left home or become suspicious of his wife's normal desire to fit into the family: 'Why do you encourage them by wearing those shorts? You know what boys are like', 'I don't want you going into their bedrooms, they may get the wrong idea.'

The children are likely to have their own ideas about the new mate and can easily set the whole thing up to make sure she has a hard time. If the new husband is younger than his wife this also applies. People who remarry often believe that the children will wish to have a positive relationship with their new partner. This is a dangerous assumption that belies the reality. The children already have two parents and they are unlikely to want a third, irrespective of the quality of that parenting. The children will be more likely to plot to get the newcomer out of the way rather than embrace them.

Men are pretty naive when it comes to the subtleties of

human relationships and are therefore quite at sea in these situations. Their desire to create happy families has them placing quite unrealistic expectations on their children's behaviour. The best they should hope for is that the new partner and the children develop a working relationship; anything more is a bonus. Often the drive to push together people who have no reason to like each other alienates them all in the long run. If children want friends the last place they will look is in the home, particularly if the new partner is seen to be replacing someone they love. Their friends will be their peers and their adult relationships will tend to be with people who will treat them as equals. Much of the conflict between the children and the new partner goes on beyond the view of the parent: 'Why are you in tears?', 'Oh, it's nothing', 'What have they been doing now? I'm fed up with having to referee between you and the kids. You'll just have to be less sensitive.' What he's unaware of is the children's desire to make his new wife look bad in his eyes. Children can be devilishly skilled in setting her up. Many women give up, accepting that the children have won the heart and mind of their father. The only way to cope with this is to change the expectations. The father needs to tell the children that he doesn't expect them to be friends with his wife; if it happens well and good but it's not a requirement. The problem is that many men remarry without admitting to themselves that they want a housekeeper and caregiver for the children. Particularly if he has teenage daughters, he feels they need a woman to deal with. His daughters may have quite a different view, particularly if the bond with their father is good. They may see themselves as not only capable of looking after themselves, but of looking after their father, too. The new wife will be stepping into a very dangerous situation if she fails to realise the competition she will encounter. She is doubly disadvantaged by the fact that the daughter knows the family rules and habits. ('We don't do it like that, Dad always has his toast buttered while it's hot.')

Men remarrying into a family with children also take on a very difficult task. Often the unconscious motivation is the replacement of their last family, to belong to a family again. For many men the *raison d'être* for their working life is to support a family; their need to be needed is satisfied by a family who loves them and relies on them. The loss of this through divorce and separation from their children takes the meaning out of their lives and makes it all seem purposeless.

Step-parenting is a difficult task at the best of times. It is made much harder when the step-parent carries unrealistic expectations. Ignoring past mistakes can lead stepfathers into dangerous shark-infested waters. Believing that he wasn't a good enough father to his own children, and missing the former contact with them, he can launch himself into getting to know the new family and being a better father to these children than their own, who doesn't seem to care for them very much, because he doesn't have much contact. His enthusiasm is probably his greatest enemy. The children will probably resent his intrusion in the first place and, secondly, react badly to his unintentional, implied criticism of their father. Family loyalties can be very strong and children can become very defensive of the absent parent if they perceive any attempt by this 'blow in' to alienate their affection. This behaviour bears no relationship to the way they treat their natural father; they are allowed to treat him badly, but heaven help any outsider who tries to do the same.

If stepfathers can curb their natural desire to create instant families, they may have a chance of developing good friendships with their stepchildren over time.

WIDOWHOOD

> My first wife died in an accident twenty years ago, and I suppose I've put her on a pedestal. I've been with other women but it never seems good enough.

Whilst it is true that women tend to outlive their husbands by five to ten years, there are still significant numbers of widowers whose lives are truncated by the death of their wives. As a man is so often eased through the pain of major emotional events in his life by his wife, the death of the very person who softened his pain leaves him bereft, lost and bewildered. Some men have resources either within themselves or around them that will take on this task, but for a good many the effort is too much and they retreat into themselves. As one group member stated 'I don't create a comfortable space, I live in the space that my wife provides, I move through it with little need to make it more than functional. When we moved I would have been happy to live out of boxes.'

In the young, these habits — whilst being antisocial — are relatively harmless, but in the elderly they can be very dangerous. The widower can make himself oblivious to his surroundings, failing to feed himself or dress or wash, retreating further into his own world, mesmerised by the television or radio and creating a world where he is not required to participate except as a spectator. He resents the intrusion of the outside world, the real world, preferring instead the cosiness of his grief.

Fortunately, this is not a typical picture. Many men are forced to re-evaluate the future after the loss of their wives, and they can see beyond the loss. For the man who is able to take the step back into the world of the living, the prospects for a rich and rewarding life may be very attractive. Men certainly have it made when it comes to prospective new partners. The widower in his fifties or sixties or even seventies will be surrounded by women and in the last age group he will be outnumbered at least two to one. As he gets older, this will become at least five to one. He becomes hot property, in great demand from women who are themselves unattached and lonely, lacking companionship and affection, sex, someone to belong to. (I have been told of a retirement village where the competition between the women for the outnumbered men became so fierce that the women decided that the men would be rationed at the weekly dance with a strict roster being maintained; whether the rostering extended beyond the dance floor I did not enquire.) We are seeing an increase in the number of marriages between people who, only ten years ago, would have been written off as being past it. The elderly seem to be taking their lives into their own hands and showing us all that happiness is not the sole property of the young and beautiful.

Sense and order are essential components of our feeling of well-being. Depression is often characterised by a loss of the sense of mastery over our own lives, the feeling that no matter what we do it won't make a blind bit of difference. The loss of a wife who has traditionally been responsible for making the house a home can result in a man who in all other respects is a capable person, quite able to fend for himself, dropping his bundle in the home. If he has relied on her for the food in the cupboard and clean clothes in the drawers, he may start camping in his own house, using one plate and cup, wearing the same clothes, never making the bed, living in one room, sleeping in the chair. This behaviour is often alarming to the family who see it as frightening evidence that Dad has given up. From his point of view, it looks quite different. He sees himself economising on effort. To a large extent men are socialised by women. When his wife is no longer there, what's the point? She would say, 'You're not going out in those shorts, are you?' and he'd go and change.

It's not just the end of a marriage, but the end of a long-standing partnership in which the tasks were reciprocal: 'I'll do this for you and you do that for me.' Even though in theory both were capable of doing most things, common sense dictated a division of labour in which each took responsibility for certain things. When a wife is no longer there, her tasks remain largely untouched, as do his. When he dies first his toolshed is likely to become draped in cobwebs with the tools rusting in their boxes, except for those occasions when she needs a hammer or a nail.

Another way of dealing with the loss is to enshrine the lost mate so that the house becomes a museum to her memory. Their real life is rewritten to idealise their qualities and obliterate their faults: 'No one could ever replace my Margaret.' Whilst this can be an initial healthy reaction to the loss of a loved one, it becomes problematic as a lifestyle. An important question is 'What do you think your partner would like you to do now?' This will often reveal that what the bereaved husband is dealing with is uncertainty about getting out into the world again and meeting people. Men are expected to be the initiators, and after twenty or thirty or forty years of marriage it takes a lot of courage to go out and put yourself on the line. The habits of singlehood have been lost years ago.

Men who are widowed young whilst still working will have the advantage of their jobs as an anchor in their lives so that work can become a point of focus. This, however, is a double-edged sword, as it often leads men into concealing their grief, having to pull themselves together for the sake of the children or to get on with work, without due regard for the consequences to themselves.

THE WORKING MAN

> For me, work is for life. But for my wife, it's optional. It never occurs to me that I have choices.

For men, the concepts of work and identity are inseparable: I am what I do. Almost the first words spoken between men meeting for the first time will include some reference to what they do for a living. And generally jobs, trades, professions and occupations carry images of lifestyle, education, values and behaviours; they help us to categorise people. It doesn't matter how accurately our picture of the job matches the person; that prejudice will colour our relationship with them, so that the person becomes what he does.

This enormous reliance on work as a measure of a man's personal worth produces more problems than it solves. For most men, their place of work provides a structure — the position they hold in the organisation, the rate of pay, the perks, the degree of challenge, the quality of the relationships with workmates and with the boss — that forms a large part of their self-concept. And when promotions come, when new responsibilities and challenges are given and wages increased, the tendency is to increase one's investment in the company, thereby reducing investment in other things, such as family and leisure. Under these circumstances the degree of dependence on the job or on the career for self-definition becomes dangerously high. The risk of job loss and consequently the loss of identity or value can become a spur for increased commitment and workload.

Since the demise of piecework and incentive schemes

in most industries, the shop floor has ceased to pit worker against worker in direct competition. Collective bargaining has given them a far less individually competitive environment. Certainly this does not apply in the world of management, where the competition can be fierce and ruthless. And it is in this jungle-like setting that many of masculinity's least desirable traits can be found. Most of the characteristics that will make men winners in the corporate world are antithetical to family life.

> For me, it's very hard to switch off when I get home. I spend my day saving my arse, watching for the guy next to me, using the tricks I've learned over the years about how to stay ahead of the game. It takes a while to drop that when I get home in the evening.

Outsiders rarely understand that, for companies, standing still is almost impossible. Most organisations have a continuous process of replenishment taking place, new people coming up, the old and incompetent moving out. Ambitious outside people are attracted to organisations that are seen as dynamic, and so the pressure develops. This high level of competition brings with it substantial stress, though it also produces rewards for the winners (and loss of value and position for the losers). But the need to turn in a better performance than your colleagues is isolating.

When men start to enter their forties and fifties, the need to keep up with technological and other innovation is often a constant source of anxiety. They see themselves as hanging onto their jobs by their fingernails, confronted by younger men who are more computer literate, educated in the latest methods. They see themselves struggling to keep up, reading the journals and not understanding the new jargon, reluctant to participate in discussions in case they show their ignorance, aware that learning new techniques and ideas can be harder at forty-five than it was at twenty-five. Under these circumstances, work can be more threatening than rewarding and lead to the threatened becoming defensive, attacking newcomers and their ideas and thereby sealing their own fate.

The fear of being too old, failing in life's goals, is very real in those areas of employment where physical risk is a large part of the job. Building, mining, commercial fishing, farming, forestry — all are industries in which the male ethos is very strong. The relationship betwen a man's usefulness, his toughness, his resilience and his age is direct, so the 'heroic' aspects of maleness will come to the fore. (They are also, incidentally, industries regarded as strong and heroic in advertisements, particularly on television.) The threat of loss of value through not being able to keep up, again provides a strong incentive to push oneself and in this way repress any fears and doubts. Moreover, when the worker is valued for his muscle rather than his intellect or creativity, the assumption is frequently made that this is all he has to offer. If this assumption is reinforced, the worker can begin to believe it is valid: 'If I am what I do and I do hard physical work, then by definition when I can no longer compete I am nothing.' The question of who he is when he is no longer strong is never asked. Very often, intellectual, emotional and creative potential lie dormant unless the man chooses to employ those assets outside his working life.

It is interesting to note that those industries that require a high degree of artistic and creative endeavour have a percentage of homosexuals out of proportion to their distribution in society. If we accept the estimate that between 5 and 7 per cent of Australia's population are homosexual, their representation in the arts and fashion, service and performance industries is obviously much higher than that. Does this mean that gay men are by nature more creatively talented than heterosexuals, or do they choose to express their creativity because their strong group identity — a product of their alienation from the 'straight' male norm — allows them to be themselves? Gay men who work in these creative industries may be expressing their creativity because they have been given permission to do so, rather than because they are gay.

The need to earn a living is central to our social structure and if a nation has 10 per cent of its workforce unemployed, it probably has at least twice that percentage feeling insecure about their own jobs — looking over their shoulders to see who is next to get the chop. Unemployment — the sword of Damocles that hangs over the heads of all employees, as bankruptcy does over the self-employed — erodes a person's ego faster than any other social disruption. At times of high unemployment even the threat of being 'laid off' or 'retrenched' or 'outpositioned' can have repercussions that spread far beyond the workplace.

Because of the stigma of unemployment and the loss of face, being retrenched often leads to a sense of failure and guilt. The victim can see himself as having in some inexplicable way contributed to his present situation, and self-doubt is very ready to appear when there is plenty of time for contemplation. 'Should I have seen the writing on the wall earlier and got out?', 'Should I have stayed at school and got a trade or a degree, or another degree, or saved more?' The opportunities for self-dissection and condemnation are endless, and the potential for depression is high, unless the person is quickly re-employed. Mild paranoia is also common, so the family's comments about lack of money in even the mildest form are likely to induce guilt in the breadwinner, leading to further reduction in self-value.

So for a great many men, the notions of independence and autonomy are conditional on the economic reality of full and secure employment — and autonomy is problematical without self-awareness, which is hardly encouraged in the workplace, as we have seen. For men to attain these goals, they need to take responsibility for their own mental health and to question the viability of being primary breadwinner and head of the family.

> We argue a lot about schools and I feel mean because I won't pay the school fees to send them to a private school. Pat insists that they should have the same chances she had but I know I'll be on the treadmill and working longer hours and frankly I'm not prepared to make the sacrifice.

Responsibility for the financial well-being of the family can impose a burden on the breadwinner that is both satisfying and frightening. The knowledge that the family live comfortably as a result of his endeavours produces a powerful incentive to succeed. While the needs of the family may not be the sole motivation for the drive towards success, however, they certainly provide a substantial rationale to justify its continuance. As long as they can convince themselves that their families expect them to continue to increase the level of goodies year by year — better school, more clothes, better holidays, bigger house — the less they need to examine the other motivations, such as power, status and challenge.

The need for men to re-evaluate this rationale is overdue. Men fail to see the connection between their family's willingness to enjoy the material benefits of their labour and their own absence from the family. In too many families, nobody ever asks at the outset just what is wanted from the husband or father: how the rest of the family feels about the trade-off between more time and fewer goodies. In most families where this is a problem, a lifestyle has already been established, with increasing expectations of the father's success, so his complaints about ungrateful kids who take for granted everything he provides will lead nowhere. Having established the pattern of being a human cheque book in the first place, he can hardly be surprised if his proposals to get out of the rat race, buy a little farm somewhere, and so on, are greeted as just more of Dad's ravings. This happens despite the fact that in many households wives contribute substantially to the family finances by their own work.

The desire to give children a good start in life should be evaluated by criteria other than material. When men value themselves more for their intrinsic qualities rather than by what they do, they may be willing to put themselves, rather than their money, at the disposal of their partners and children.

RETIREMENT

> I've seen my parents struggling to keep a decent standard of living. But when the money gets short and they stay at home, they don't seem to have anything to say to each other.

A useful measure of the impact of paid work on men's identity can be gauged through a study of their general reaction to retirement.

The differences between men's expectations of retirement and the reality are quite marked. For most men, retirement is characterised by two issues: giving up work (which is seen positively) and eking out a living on inadequate resources (which is seen negatively). The rationale usually goes something like this: I've worked hard all my life, and I'm glad I'm getting a break at last. We'll go on a trip, I'll play golf, play bowls. We'll get a smaller place up the coast, or in the bush. And we'll invest our super and I can do odd jobs to provide little luxuries. Life will be one long holiday until we die.

If only that were the truth.

Four major issues need to be addressed at retirement.

These are people, leisure, health and financial security. The first two have been largely ignored, while the last two dominate; understandably, their dominance in the retirement debate overshadows the significance of the other two. It is interesting to note that the popularly accepted definition of a retirement plan is exclusively financial. Newspapers, magazines, banks and building societies all promote the idea that planning for retirement is all about inflation, property, cash management trusts, dividends, and so on.

But the link between work and people and work and leisure must be understood if retirees are to receive the rewards of a lifetime's paid employment. Most men in the workforce have spent more than half their working lives in the company of their workmates — more time than they spend with any other group of people, including wives and children. It is with workmates that these common experiences are shared, that roles are defined, that group identity is established. There are shared jokes, routines, relationships, values, skills, even enemies — all these things state who the man is and how he is seen. This definition is often quite different from the identity that men have with their families and with outside friends, and the roles will often be incompatible.

The loss of paid work means the loss of these relationships, so a loss of a certain role and identity. When a man says he is retired, he does not mention these losses, or missing people, feeling less valuable, not knowing what to do with his time, or what to talk to his partner about.

Which brings us to the second issue, leisure. When we as a society have great difficulty in enjoying our leisure time creatively during our working lives, why should we think we can magically transform ourselves into consumers of creative leisure in retirement?

You can see the results of this in any suburban supermarket, with men wandering around, doing the shopping with their wives, or sitting in the sun or doing the gardening. These pursuits, while admirable in themselves, hardly represent a lifestyle. As a result, too many people grow old before their time, not because they have worked too hard but because they are bored, they feel a sense of loss of purpose, lack of relevance, observers rather than participants. For men who are trained to be doers, this sense of being discarded is particularly hard to adjust to, and for too many men the consequence is depression.

Of course, they are not *supposed* to feel depressed, but to rejoice. After all, work is something negative we do for most of our lives, and leisure is what we do with the spaces in between. It naturally follows that, when you have finished work, the balance of life is leisure: you have given up the bad and taken up the good.

The trouble with these concepts is that they are laid down in the early part of people's lives. Schooling and being young seem so precious that starting a career that will last a lifetime seems like a tremendous sacrifice. At the end of a person's working life these views may be quite changed: work may represent a measure of achievement, competence, a place to belong, to find friendship, respect and value.

A man is giving up a setting in which he has prestige and a role, for a place — home — where he may have neither. For many men, the home is his wife's domain, as it has been for years, and he must fit into her routine. Neither he nor she is prepared for the intrusion that his retirement will represent to her ordered life. Instead of waving him off at the door, she finds him beside her in the kitchen asking for a cup of tea when it's at least an hour before she has her morning coffee. Many men would rather not be hanging around at home . . . but if they can't even be useful there, then where are they?

One of the great difficulties men experience is the ability to play. Almost all male activities need to be purposeful: if there is no end result, nothing concrete to show, then what is the point of doing anything?

Most male leisure activities that are active (as opposed to passive, such as watching sport or television) have an end product. Much of the work I do with men is getting them to play in such a way that the activity is its own reward. This is how children play; they have little or no regard for long-term results, and the pleasure is in the moment. I get men to do a painting and throw it away, or to make a totally impractical clay object, throw it away and start again. This makes quite a lot of men uncomfortable, because it is totally foreign to the concept that you should have something to show for your labours. But it is a way of trying to teach them to enjoy the present, rather than anticipating the future.

I know how difficult this can be sometimes. My hobby is cabinet making, from which I derive great satisfaction, yet I have a continual battle with myself to enjoy the moment, to participate totally in the activity without anticipating what the piece will be like on completion and how long it will take to finish.

If men are to enjoy their retirement, they have to get themselves into a frame of mind where they are enjoying what they do, not mourning the loss of paid work. It's the time when men can do things they've always wanted to: painting, courses in world politics, studying Spanish, or music. Adjustment is needed, but retirement can and should be a time when any new mental direction is possible.

MEN TOGETHER

> Women are more responsive to expressions of feeling and emotion than men. I'd be much more likely to express my deep feelings to women because I experience them as understanding.

> I've got loads of business colleagues but none that I'd call mates. Mostly they come and go; there's a turnover of them but over time nothing sticks. No close friendships ever result.

When pressed to talk about real friendships, those based on mutual trust that have endured for a long time, men will admit they have friends with whom they do things, and friends of longstanding. But they rarely reveal their true selves to these friends. For most, the relationship is based on doing rather than being, and they avoid dealing with personal issues in their lives, particularly weakness and failures. This being the case, they will certainly not discuss them with other men, as their competitiveness will not permit them to. As Donald Horne wrote in *The Lucky Country*:

> There is a wider, but still exclusive sense, in which mateship is simply comradeship within a male fraternity. There is a socially homosexual side to Australian male life (of a 'butch' kind) that can involve prolonged displays of toughness in male company. Men stand around bars asserting their masculinity with such intensity that you half expect them to unzip their flies.

Men hunger for the kinds of friendships they believe women have with each other. But they have been brought up to be competitive, and friendship of this kind results only when both parties are prepared to be open, vulnerable, with each other. This goes right against the grain for many men. Not only this, they fear closeness with other men because of possible homosexual overtones and potential for hurt, and they question their ability to relate to each other. Many men are unable to articulate their hunger for intimacy clearly, as few of them have ever experienced it in adult life.

Here we must return to the issue of the father/son relationship and its impact on man's perceived ability for emotional closeness. Boys and girls both need touching, warmth, cuddles and emotional expression, as any parent will attest. Yet when we see boys and girls in late primary school, their behaviour towards each other is markedly different. Boys will be fighting and competing, while girls will be much more likely to interact with each other in less aggressive ways. What have boys done with the needs they had five or six years ago? Have they been satisfied, sublimated or repressed, converted into aggressive rather than empathic supportive energy?

A common response to emotional loss or stress in children is to play with their genitals to derive comfort from self-pleasure. Boys masturbate at an early age more often than girls and, while this could be said to derive from the fact that male sexual organs are external, perhaps boys learn at an early age that their gradual loss of emotional connectedness with their parents, particularly with their fathers, can be compensated for by masturbation. The penis becomes an organ for emotional expression. In 'The Masculine Mystique', Frank Pittman writes:

> A boy's penis seems so enormous and hard to hide, far too big yet too small, always too small. It has a life of its own, responding to all the wrong things at the wrong times, intrusive and embarrassing, yet utterly honest in its responses.

> It requires much time and attention, much measuring, exploration and comparison with the other guys, and much concern about how it is going to behave in the presence of girls. The boy has little control over it, and for a few years it is not clear who is in charge of whom. He must masturbate constantly to keep it down. But beat it down, however many times a day, and it will spring back up just when it is least expected. Yet when it is needed it is nowhere to be found; with any anxiety it will run away and hide. The boy has become one of Siamese twins, with this other independent being attached to his body, a constant, unreliable companion, a source of comfort and entertainment when alone, but a steady embarrassment in public.

Women often say that the only time their partners seem to express significant emotion is when they want sex, or that any expression of warmth or tenderness on the part of the woman is seen by the man as an invitation to bed. They may see men as obsessed by sex and, in truth, men are frequently trapped by this sublimation of their emotions into their sexuality.

If men's emotional responses tend to be focused in their sexual expression, then the whole idea of male–male intimacy becomes very threatening to heterosexual men. Long gone are the masturbation contests, with all the shame they invoke: all that remains is a sense of disquiet at the prospect of getting close, touching other men with tenderness.

It starts to make sense that men experience their greatest intimacy, friendship and willingness to die for each other when the going is tough: that is the time when they are safe from their sexual urges and desires. The situation is not conducive to sensual tenderness; on the contrary, this is probably the last thing on their minds.

Most examples we see of men addressing the issue of their emotional distance from each other are probably far removed from the everday lives of most men. Groups, counselling, etc., though useful, probably do not markedly change men's lives or their relationships with other men. Given a protected environment and a common purpose, we can all attempt new behaviours and take risks. A men's group can uncover a deep well of longing for a new way of relating, and men can experience the emotional high of seeing each other as they really are when they put aside their armour. But this hasn't happened in the workplace, the family, or the sports field, or the pub, so those few men who take a step towards each other find themselves confined to the hothouse, like rare tropical plants that require a special controlled environment in order to bloom, and that would wither and die on the outside.

When looked at superficially, the problem of opening the hearts and minds of men to each other seems overwhelming. But it may not be so daunting if the goals are modest. We can be encouraged by the fact that there is a high degree of dissatisfaction among men about their relationships that is largely unexpressed. It is often directed towards women, particularly among men whose marriages have ended, and this can also be seen in the backlash against some more extreme elements of the women's movement. But it is often easier (and safer) to blame women for the problem than to look to ourselves for solutions. Men must first recognise the true nature of their sense of discontent in order to begin to do something about it, and a start in this process can be made only if it is seen to be important, not anti-woman and relatively safe.

HOMOSEXUALITY

> I often speculate on what my life would have been like if I hadn't been gay. I used to feel as though I'd been cursed, that it was some kind of punishment. Now, that I have accepted it, I just am, and I like myself.

The Australian male's homophobia has more to do with his fear of intimacy with other males than with the sexual practices of homosexuals. It is linked to his fear of losing his selfhood, which is anchored in his concept of masculinity.

By and large, most heterosexual men are tolerant of gays: 'I don't care what they do as long as it doesn't affect me'. The fiercely homophobic adults tend to be drawn from the fringes of society, rather than the mainstream, whereas teenage homophobia is more likely to be symptomatic of more complex teenage issues.

But many people still believe that homosexuality can be caught, like the measles, and so to them the gay pedophile is the lowest of the low. In some men's eyes, such a person not only violates a child but by the same act turns him into a homosexual: which they see as abhorrent.

I believe that many heterosexuals feel uncomfortable with the sexual practices of gay men. Oral sex doesn't seem odd; perhaps they engage in it themselves with their wives and girlfriends, but anal intercourse is something else: that's unnatural. And for the first time, heterosexual men are starting to encounter aggressive gays, which challenges their view that these guys are okay as long as they don't bother me.

A father's fear of his son becoming gay is less likely to result from an aversion to homosexuality as such than from a strong belief that the life of a gay man is very difficult; he belongs to a persecuted minority, and is cut off from the mainstream of life.

> I feel really stuck. When I see my fourteen-year-old son waving his arms about and putting on that walk I think, oh my God, he's going to be gay. I feel that if I tell him about my fears, it will only make things worse. Rationally I know that if he is there is nothing I can do about it, but this doesn't stop me from trying to change his behaviour. I imagine the

> other kids giving him hell. I remember what it was like to be different when I was a boy and I don't want it to happen to him.

Consequently, parents are likely to feel a conflict between their liberal, rational selves and their emotions. A father's anxiety for his son's sexual identity is likely to be expressed in a number of ways. He may say to his son 'Why don't you get out more, play more sport?' or criticise his choice of friends, activities, or lack of girlfriends. What he is doing is strengthening the bond between the boy and his mother, who will see this as unwarranted criticism of a sensitive son. Further, the son will also feel alienated from his father and question his own value in his father's eyes, thus leading to further problems of identity and inadequacy.

The changes that have taken place and the increased acceptance of homosexuals' right to exist have certainly improved their lot considerably over the past twenty years. Yet it is still true that if the behaviour that has been — and still is — meted out to homosexuals were to be applied to any other minority, racial, ethnic, cultural or religious group, there would be a national outcry. There is a lot of fear about homosexuality in the 'straight' community, and this is difficult to understand rationally. There is a perception among men whose chief expression of emotion lies in their sexuality that only men who love and have sex with women are real men; the others are neuter. Men can't be men and gay at the same time, no matter how butch they may be. A man's masculinity seems to be determined by his choice of sexual partner, regardless of the other aspects of his personality. Furthermore, the power of gay radicals to bring other gays to their knees with the threat of 'outing' is a measure of the relative superficiality of the community acceptance there is. The result is that a far greater number of hidden gays exist than have ever come out: if you add to these numbers the bisexuals and transvestites who fear exposure, the depth of the problem begins to emerge.

> There's a hell of a difference between being gay in the city and gay in the country. I was raised out west in a small country town in New South Wales. I knew I was gay from the time I was fourteen or fifteen, but there was no way I could ever let on. I had to pretend for the next eight years that I was just like everybody else. At times it seemed like a choice between life and death. I came to Sydney and now I belong, but I had to lose my family in the process. My father has never spoken to me since I left home. It's as if I had never existed.

When talking to gay men, one can see the problems that homosexuality poses, particularly for those who will never come out. Their lives are lived in constant fear of exposure — they examine their every gesture, voice tone, stance and topic of conversation for signs of self-betrayal. It is endless, an excruciating process of self-observation.

The outsider may ask 'Why does this have to be so? Why don't they just come out and stop the pretence? Surely it would be better in the long run.' But many of these people have built their lives on their ability to conceal their inbuilt drives. Family, friends and career are threatened if they drop the mask. The potential to hurt others is usually the main rationale for continuing the deception, compounded by the expectation that they will be rejected by those they love.

Some people find great difficulty in accepting that a man can have a wife and children and still be homosexual or transvestite; the popular perception is that homosexuals' sexual preference in some way leads them to reject the opposite sex. Nothing could be further from the truth. People confuse sexuality with friendship or love. If we could love only those towards whom we felt a sexual drive, what a bleak and impoverished world it would be! Men and women frequently remark on the comfort they feel when relating to gays of the opposite gender. They are generally seen as non-threatening.

But there are still so many myths, so many hidden fears about homosexuality. And many gays feel that, just as they were beginning to gain acceptance and respectability in the community, the AIDS epidemic has handed homophobes a ready-made weapon with which to fight them. They are currently attacked by some fundamentalist groups as the carriers of a dreadful disease, a consequence of their unsavoury habits, further justifying their self-righteous and violent attacks on the gay community.

We know, however, that the unwillingness of a society to accept homosexuality can have dire consequences. One has to look no further than the state and federal governments of the US, who refused to accept the explosive spread of sexually transmitted AIDS in the gay community by not funding public awareness campaigns. The government's criminal irresponsibility and neglect of a massive social epidemic undoubtedly contributed to the spread of the disease and the resulting deaths of thousands of innocent people. In Australia, public awareness is much higher, though there is little room for complacency.

If we take homosexuality to be the manifestation of a biological difference in sexual preference — and *only* that — we can begin to expect homosexuals' collective and individual attitudes to be no different from those of the rest of society. Their community will include criminals, geniuses, pedophiles, the monogamous, the promiscuous, the shy, the bold, the introverted and the extroverted. The sensationalism and controversy that tends to follow the gay community ensures the perpetuation of the distance separating homosexual and heterosexual men. Heterosexual men must examine their fears and admit them, labelling them for what they are, before they can hope to accept homosexual men as part of the brotherhood. Perhaps these same fears drive the zealots and religious bigots of our society. And perhaps we can encourage them to examine their own motivations.

SPORT

> There's a spirit in the Wallabies
> Mere words cannot describe,
> It's as if they had descended
> From some legendary tribe.
> There's a kinship, a tradition
> As in days so long since past
> Of crusades, of knights in armour
> And of men before the mast.
>
> Peter Fenton, Sydney football coach

What are the main leisure pursuits of Australian men?

Watching sport on television would have to be high on the list (probably followed by watching sport live, playing sport, having social outings, barbecues, drinking with mates, working on the car or in the garden, watching the kids play sport, and going to the beach).

This interest in sport brings out what are regarded as significantly male characteristics; either as a spectator or participant, sport is characterised by highly aggressive tests of courage, strength, skill, endurance and determination. To stand at the wicket with a bat and one's reflexes as the only protection, facing a bowler delivering a ball at up to 100 kilometres per hour, requires great skill and nerve. And the spectator who watches the batsman do so, will feel strong and courageous by proxy. Men are likely to say 'My team won' as if responsible for this success. Sportsmen carry the colours of men's egos.

In fact, sport is such an integral part of man's identity that those men who have little or no interest in watching it or participating in it will question their maleness — or if they don't, other men will! My own rites of passage to being male were severely delayed because I had asthma and was not able to run, jump or catch a ball. I lacked practice, so I had little coordination and therefore confidence. When a ball was thrown to me, my heart would pound and I would know that no matter how hard I concentrated it would hit me or bounce out of my hands. Then I would have to mumble the standard apology and feel ashamed. Mostly the other boys would say nothing — they would even act as if I was not there. Even telling about it these days, I wince. The situation was relieved somewhat when my father took me to athletic meetings and the occasional rugby match when I was in my early teens. This gave me access; if I couldn't play sport, at least I could talk about it. Now I could dispel the notion that I wasn't a real man!

Because the media recognise men's need to identify with heroes, they have saturated the airwaves with sport, both in full descriptions of matches and news about games, and in advertisements that use sportsmen to endorse a range of products (mainly, it has to be said, beer, that other masculine icon).

This male preoccupation with sport has both advantages and disadvantages. On the positive side, it can promote health, provide a setting for non-destructive aggression, develop a person's reflexes and mental agility, promote excellence through competition, develop cooperative effort through teamwork, engender a sense of achievement, teach people to conquer their fears, gain mastery over their weaknesses and structure leisure time. It's a pretty substantial list.

Furthermore, watching sport fulfils some important needs in men. Not only does being a spectator provide entertainment but also an outlet for emotions that otherwise would remain unexpressed. A woman may ask 'Why are you so grumpy? It's only a lost football match.'

Has she no heart? Doesn't she realise how *important* this is? Watch a group of male spectators and see the massive range of emotions expressed as the team's fortunes wax and wane. In no other setting would such raw feelings be likely to see the light of day. And the ability to identify with the players can even give the impression that in some magical way the spectator contributed to the outcome. (Whenever my youngest son and I sit up to watch the late night soccer, my wife always ends up asking us to keep our voices down so she can get some sleep. Many a night we have carried the fortunes of the whole team on our shoulders, helped the referee and advised the coach without moving out of our armchairs.)

The down side of sport is that it can promote intolerance and ethics can be supplanted by the need to win at any cost. Sport also lends itself to becoming a vehicle for national and group hostilities — one has only to think of the Olympic Games. The competition can stifle men's cooperative and vulnerable side. For too many men, golf, tennis or squash is an extension of their working life so that the drive to win, to improve the game, becomes the main objective. A beautiful golf course is not seen for its beauty but for its obstacles. What is often lacking is the ability to relax and to enjoy the experience for its own sake; this is a problem men have, as we have noticed before. No sensible person would suggest that we improve on our picnic skills or our bushwalking times, yet so much sport is played like this. Men's need for doing rather than being traps them again and again.

As we said in the chapter about retirement and leisure, it is men's inability to play, to enjoy themselves, to suspend self-consciousness, to *let go*, that stifles many areas of self-expression. Too often men equate creativity with output rather than input; they are likely to expect that creativity should result in a concrete object that has value and purpose. This is why so many Anglo-Celtic

Australian men feel alarmed at the idea of getting up and dancing. Few have enough sense of their own bodies to be free enough to dance with grace and rhythm. Visit a dance hall and observe the men venturing onto the floor; they look either like articulated puppets or deep sea divers. They just won't let go.

Yes, some men say, but I don't have the capacity to do any of that stuff. But are Welshmen born with better voices than Australian men? Do black people have a greater sense of rhythm than whites? The ability to sing and dance is inherent in all human beings; while some will undoubtedly be better than others, it is not talent that inhibits us but permission and encouragement.

The ability to derive satisfaction and pleasure from self-generated activities that have little outward purpose has been substantially eroded in the last fifty years; prepackaged entertainment has to some degree become a substitute. I think this is a great pity.

We cannot hope to consider the question of maleness without looking at man's relationship with those symbols of his male potency — cars, bikes, and guns.

Of course, these were all preceded by the horse. A man astride a spirited horse — a powerful animal that had been mastered and tamed — has been used for centuries as representing power and achievement. (How many equestrian statues are there in European and Australian cities, for instance?) The advertising industry was certainly not unaware of the symbolism, using the man on a horse to sell countless cigarettes to generations of boys who would be men.

But now men have replaced the horse with even more powerful objects to enhance their perception of their masculinity. The motorbike is a direct descendant of the horse, with the advantages that it is more powerful, faster and is more accessible to all, rich or poor. If you want to see the cult of masculinity in action, look at the Hells Angels. They epitomise the most extreme limits of macho behaviour. Everything about them screams raw sexual power: their bikes, dress, lifestyle, relationships with women exemplify Goths or Huns rather than twentieth-century men. The bikies' machines are as sacred as the phalluses they represent.

The car is a somewhat less obvious sex symbol, yet it gives the driver great status. What is the difference between a Ferrari and a VW, apart from the price? They are both means of transport. Yet the statement the Ferrari makes about its owner is very definite. The logo of the Ferrari is a rampant stallion, for a start. Besides, the car's shape is phallic. The driver reclines in it, confident in the statement he is making to women and to other men.

Petrolheads are the modern gladiators, competing to see who burns most rubber at the lights, showing off, challenging, getting high on adrenalin, drawing attention to themselves. And just like the ancient knights, they compete for the favours of women.

Men and cars have been engaged in a love affair ever since men walked in front of them carrying red flags. But perhaps we should have realised that this was not to warn other road users of the danger, but to warn men that they ran the risk of being captured and enslaved by this new machine.

At least horses lived and breathed, had personalities, frailties and strengths. Men could relate to them. But the car, on the other hand, asks for nothing but money and a bit of mechanical care. No interaction is needed for it to work; it would carry out the same tasks no matter who was at the controls, and could just as easily be driven by a robot as by a living person.

There is considerable debate over the environmental problems that the private car produces, but rarely are the social problems addressed. The relationship between men and their cars needs re-examination. Men need to be aware that things — inanimate objects such as cars, computers, robots, may have the potential to free people from mindless tedious tasks and to save time, but at the same time they can become substitutes for people. Men who are already orientated to the external, to things, to doing, can easily be seduced into seeing machines — including cars — as an answer to the problems in their lives.

This is true of computers, too. At least when someone wanted a game of chess or cards in the past, other people had to be involved. Now, with interactive computers, all this can be done without having to speak to another human being, or to deal with their disappointment or elation when the game is completed. The computer is eternally patient, understanding and rewarding. Real people, on the other hand, are likely to sulk, or make excuses, or hold a post mortem about how they should have won. But this is the real world!

This process of distancing is nowhere more apparent than in the area of guns and warfare. As we look at the development of weapons, we can see that the gradual process of distancing a person from the consequences of his actions is almost completed. As the Gulf War so graphically demonstrated, with the diagrams on late-night television, we are now in a position to kill people we never see. We can also hit targets from around the world with pinpoint accuracy. The gun in all its forms gives people the power to demand obedience, and the culture of guns and weapons represents a serious threat to men's hopes for connectedness. The gun is the ultimate alienator, providing a setting for the very type of macho maleness men need to leave behind.

MEN AND POWER

> Power isn't all it's cracked up to be. I'd give it away tomorrow if the system would let me. Women should try taking all the burden and see what it's like.

Power is an essential aspect of our needs, both as individuals and as a society; the lack of a sense of personal power can lead to depression and low self-esteem. In order to feel valuable we need to have a sense of mastery over our own lives, to believe that we are in some way able to influence the events that dictate them.

Seen at a social level, the use of power and its consequent negative effect both on the powerful and the powerless serve to reinforce the belief that it is power per se that is the problem. The negative consequences of power can be seen in numerous examples: the failure of men to ordain women; some police attitudes towards Aborigines; attitudes of the legal profession towards rape victims.

The statement is often made that women exercise power differently from men: they aren't power hungry, so would handle positions of influence better. In short, if the instruments of power were given to women, the world would be a better place. Women's natural desire for consensus and their need to nurture would be translated into creative decisions that would shape our society. Unfortunately, this assumption is highly questionable; present evidence seems to indicate that women have been no more effective in promoting social values than have been their male counterparts.

Two factors reduce the likelihood of women being able

to transform society by wresting power from men. Firstly, by their very nature, institutions will transform the values and attitudes of the people who join them, and secondly, the process by which some are drawn to seek power and influence will select out individuals who will display what we tend to describe as male traits: competitiveness and aggression. As long as men set the rules, those women who aspire to positions of high office will be successful only to the extent that they can demonstrate these values.

The most empowering opportunity women have is probably motherhood; it places them in a position to influence future generations more significantly than any other person. Male power, of course, is entrenched most effectively in the major institutions of our society: the legal profession, law enforcement agencies, the political arena, industry, the churches and so on . . . all the institutions that shape and control our society are dominated by men.

When considering men and power, one must begin by stating the obvious: in general, men are physically stronger and bigger than women. Perhaps because women are usually conscious of this male potential to decide any conflict or disagreement by force, they are more likely to exercise power covertly, relying on gaining influence by subtle or even manipulative means.

When I think of my own parents, I realise that the pattern of interaction that led to decision making was ingrained. Superficially my father was the boss and my mother the follower — yet it was Mum who controlled the direction of the family's future. This was a sort of open secret, never spoken of, but obvious all the same. Mum would drop hints about what she wanted to have happen; Dad would give reasoned arguments why this was not possible. Mum would say little or nothing, just wait — as would we all. When the matter was next raised the objections would be less strenuous until Mum got her way, then honour was satisfied.

> My mother used to say that she was in charge of the little things in family life . . . what we kids ate, where we went to school, what we did, how much money was spent. She said Dad looked after the really important stuff: nuclear war, the balance of payments, the economy . . .

I suppose that most men involved in this kind of situation mildly resented the fact that they lacked influence in making decisions that affected the family, perhaps feeling they were controlled by women (though uncertain of just how) but seeing little alternative.

This use of covert skills disadvantages both men and women. A classic method of trying to deal with low self-worth is to gain mastery over others by force or manipulation. In this way, the power diminishes both the wielder of the power and the victim, as the aggressor fails to address the problem of low self-worth, and the victim once more becomes the target of another's problem.

Another problem with this style of manipulative power is that it is characterised by relatively fixed views that are rarely challenged. Both men and women are robbed of the chances to discuss and evaluate the merits of various alternative proposals. The man may feel that his wife is likely to propose ill-considered schemes and that she lacks the rationality so important for decision-making; the woman may feel that he never values her ideas, feeling only the need to be right and in control, the necessity to point out the flaws in her proposition.

We need to consider the differences in ways that men and women tend to make decisions. Not surprisingly, they fall into categories that seem to represent traditional spheres of responsibility. Men favour the macro, long-term, instrumental welfare issues, while women favour the short to medium term, emotional welfare issues. Consequently, they will approach decision-making with different and rarely acknowledged perspectives.

A typical discussion may go something like this. He: 'I think we should buy a sandwich bar, the turnover would be terrific and we could both work in it and be comfortable for the rest of our lives.' (Unspoken message: 'I'm fed up with my job, I want to find some security for our future, I'm not sure I can support the family on my salary.') She: 'What are you talking about? Who would look after the baby during the day while I spent my time cutting sandwiches?' (Unspoken message: 'What a fool you are! We can hardly manage things now, let alone embarking on harebrained schemes that won't work.') He: 'You always pour cold water on my ideas. You never support me like other men's wives, you just drag me down.' And so the whole thing would probably escalate into a session of personal abuse, with both digging into their respective hurt bags to pull out the most telling stories from the past to validate their respective positions.

Men are significantly disadvantaged in these sessions; women have an incredible capacity for detailed recollection of past events. Men have poor detail recall and will tend to disbelieve women who recount events in the past with conviction, dismissing what they say as made up. Because of this difference in approach, men will often accuse women of bearing grudges and being unable to forgive and forget. Perhaps women have developed this characteristically detailed memory by necessity. Because they have the overall responsibility for the daily welfare of the family, women need to know and keep in their heads masses of data that, while apparently trivial, individually ensure the smooth functioning of the household.

Men see themselves as delegating this role to women, and consequently feel able both to distance themselves from the detail and to have expectations about its successful execution. So, while the thoughtful man will see it as right that he should help his partner with the child-rearing chores, the shopping and the cleaning, he will see her as ultimately responsible for the coordination and the outcome. Consequently, her power is subjected to his view of her power by his grace and favour.

But past hurts can often be resolved by using a counselling technique: the partners take turns to recount events in the past that they still resent. Women usually have pictures of these events that are teeming with dialogue and detail, men will be more likely to remember events in non-specific terms.

I remember counselling a couple, Kevin and Jessica, who were both forty-six and who had been married for twenty-two years. When they came for counselling they had been fighting for most of the last decade, and the atmosphere was charged with resentment. From the outset both tried to take control, vying to be heard; clearly, neither felt the other had been listening for years. Jessica's list of complaints went back to the time before they were married. She was angry that he had forgotten the first anniversary of their first date, and spoke with great sadness about his having asked his mother to look after her when she first came home with their baby because he was needed at work, as well as his having ignored her at a particular party when he was aware she knew nobody except him. On the other hand, his accusations were far more generalised, couched in such terms as 'You're cold, you never have anything nice to say to me.' His main hurt was that she would take anybody's word but his, she would ridicule his plans and took no interest in his work.

Kevin and Jessica were both apparently angry and unhappy, but in reality they had a sound relationship burdened with unresolved issues. His behaviour had denigrated her emotional world, hers did the same to his practical, future-orientated world of things. When they could feel heard and understood, the past could be resolved and the future prepared for. In a way Jessica was caught in the past because it had been unresolved for her, while he was stalled in the present because the relationship was not able to move forward.

VIOLENCE

> I feel shame and disgust about other men's reprehensible behaviour, but I don't feel guilt. I'm certainly more circumspect than I used to be, so now I avoid situations in which I may be placed in a position where my behaviour could be seen as sexual.

The fact that the institutions in our society are controlled by men, may seem to place men at an enormous advantage — all benefiting from the power of significant individuals. But this is only true if the behaviour of these men in power is seen to be positive. If they are not, they may further erode men's self-image.

Furthermore, while a handful of men wield enormous power, the bulk of them will never exercise control over much more than their children, and even then the efficacy of that influence is questionable. In general, the actual power wielded by the average bloke is more illusory than real. He is more likely to see himself as controlled than controlling, beset by demands on him that severely restrict his freedom of choice. His family's needs dictate his commitment to work, both at his place of employment and around the home, and this in turn dictates his response to his superiors at work because he needs the job. Far from feeling masters of their lives, men are more likely to feel slaves to everybody's competing needs, with themselves coming a poor last.

And sometimes violence results from the frustration that may be built up because of these feelings. This may be directed towards objects rather than towards wives or children — but for women and children the result is the same. One of the most common misunderstandings in men subject to temper outbursts is that violent behaviour towards things is almost as frightening as violence towards the person. A man will say 'I'll never touch her or the kids so I'll just punch the wall or smash something if I get really mad, and that will get it out of my system.' He may see himself acting responsibly, getting rid of his rage, but his wife and children will see a large, powerful person out of control, demonstrating his potential for violence and destruction.

> What was most destructive was not what he did but what he had the power to do.

In this society, the most potent negative symbols of male power are rape, incest and physical violence. It is impossible to address the issues of men and power without examining these shameful abuses of male power.

I find great difficulty in discussing these subjects with any reasonable degree of objectivity, since a good deal of my practice consists of working with men and women who have been the victims of these acts. People who have never worked in this field find difficulty in understanding the extent to which the victims' lives are devastated. The experience of violence permeates every aspect of their personality, impacting on their sense of personal worth, the quality of their relationships — all those things that the rest of the population take for granted. And while objectively as a therapist I can understand the circumstances that may bring a person to carry out sexually violent acts, I must leave an understanding of their behaviour to others.

Estimates of the number of women who have been abused by rape or incest range from 70 per cent of the female population to much lower figures; an accurate assessment will always be difficult to obtain in so emotionally charged and secretive an area as the family. Whether the figure is 70 per cent or 20 per cent or somewhere in between, the fact that it occurs at all is shameful; even 1 per cent is 1 per cent too many.

The background that I came from was that you knock them around and you screw them and that keeps them in their place.

It may be useful to see various sexual crimes as belonging to a continuum, with power and violence at one end and sexual inadequacy and desire at the other. For instance, voyeuristic behaviour (such as that of flashers) is largely motivated by a need for sexual expression, but inability to relate effectively to women. At the other end are the acts of sexual violence such as rape (rightly seen as an act of violence rather than one of sex) and sadistic attacks that are primarily motivated by a desire to hurt, punish, humiliate and control. The rapist embodies all the worst characteristics of masculinity: strength without compassion, sexuality without sensitivity, raw and unbridled power.

Incest probably ranges from one end of the continuum to the other, from one incident or episode of inappropriate touching or cuddling to brutal and violent sexual abuse perpetrated over years and years. In a way, it is worse than rape. Most rape is carried out by someone the victim knows; such as a husband, boyfriend, friend or relative. According to a report by Roseanne Bonney, only 28 per cent of rapes are committed by total strangers. The resulting trauma cannot be overstated, and the attack is usually seen by the victim as an attack on herself by someone who wishes to harm her. By contrast, because incest occurs within a family, it represents a massive betrayal of trust, particularly when perpetrated by a father against a daughter or son. Any act by an adult that uses his or her children as objects of sexual gratification is incestuous and extremely harmful to the child. Even if the acts seem relatively harmless to the adult — 'I was only tickling her, it was harmless, we all get drunk sometimes and do things we regret afterwards' — the child becomes aware through secrecy and the atmosphere generated that this is wrong, and by then the damage has been done. Whereas a rape victim can hope to get at least a sympathetic hearing from home and friends, the incest victim is denied this modest assurance. The place that should represent the epitome of comfort, safety and nurturance is transformed into a prison in which the victimiser holds all the power.

> I think I knew even at that age that I was on my own. As I got older I used to think at least it keeps him quiet and maybe that's all I'm worth. I had no idea the price I paid. Even at forty-five I'm still learning to live with it.

Comments like this one are frequently made by people who have been abused as children. The latent power is almost more destructive than the actual sexual acts. Unfortunately, until quite recently many children who attempted to tell their elders of their behaviour were either ignored or punished. Things are changing, and I hope we now have better understanding of appropriate responses to such tentative cries for help.

But my intention here is not to discuss in detail the whole issue of incest; this book is intended to look at maleness and men's attitudes to themselves and women. A rarely addressed aspect of the increased publicity about incest is the negative effect it has on the behaviour of ordinary men.

> I have two boys and two girls and I was horrified when my four-year-old daughter tried to kiss me by opening her mouth. We both made a joke of it but I felt acutely uncomfortable.

At one level men are being encouraged to get in touch with their feelings and to relate to their children in a softer way, to play with them, not to abandon their sons and daughters physically when they reach puberty. Yet at another level they are very anxious, even frightened, at the prospect of being guilty of inappropriate touching or being accused of this.

Nowhere is this paranoia more prevalent than when men are stepfathers. In most marriage breakups, children carry a deep desire for the father to be restored to the family. This can cause them to develop a strong dislike for any male who comes on the scene. Should the mother's new relationship develop to a point where the man moves in, his ability to relate naturally to the children will be severely inhibited by his paranoia and no doubt the children's mother will be watchful of the new man in the house. Consequently, the most ordinary gestures of warmth and affection may not be made, and the growth of a normal accepting relationship may be further inhibited.

The mere accusation of sexual abuse is a powerful weapon. Many marriages end physically but not emotionally; anger and bitterness may remain long after the legal break has been made. In a climate of claim and counter-claim, the children often become the spoils of war, with each parent asserting a superior claim to being the more effective and loving parent. And in order to verify this claim of superiority, the most effective tactic is to accuse the other of cruelty, indifference or sexual abuse. Because this charge carries such enormous social condemnation, the merest hint from an angry ex-wife is likely to cause the man to change the nature of his interaction with his children or to require a chaperone to verify his innocence — hardly a positive setting for being an effective parent.

Every day men are confronted by accounts of other men behaving in the most bestial fashion to women and children. How are they to respond to these crimes with any effectiveness? Some men take cases of sexual crimes or acts of serious domestic violence personally, as if they were responsible in some way. And they may feel an irrational need to say to women 'I'm not like that'.

In talking to men in groups, this undercurrent of

collective disquiet is very evident. The issue of sexual abuse is particularly complex; more than half of the men in one of my groups admitted to experiencing some form of sexual interference from strangers, family members or friends during childhood. So reactions to the perpetrators of these crimes was both objective and subjective, as they saw themselves both as victims and by association victimisers — needing to condemn men who abused, cope with their own feelings about their own abuse, and finally decide how they felt about being male.

To the sexual or physical abuse of male power, men's response must be a clear, unequivocal and public *no.* No amount of provocation justifies it, no excuse can be accepted, no psychological rationale can be considered adequate. Trying to minimise the occurrence or to balance the equation by citing examples of women being violent simply makes men apologists for reprehensible behaviour, and gives the perpetrators the opportunity to hide behind the delusion that other men think it is okay under certain circumstances. But the violence must stop, and we men must fight with all our strength and will to declare it unacceptable and to challenge the abusers to change.

CONCLUSION

Time does not alter men — it merely unmasks them.

Hal Porter, 'On the Ridge'

Women are anchored in their bodies by their potential for motherhood, their most fundamental creativity, and their focus is internal; men, on the other hand have an external focus. They have no such direct link with their potency. Even the penis, that slender connection with their procreative potential, is an external organ, a pathetic symbol of fecundity by comparison with women's vagina and womb.

Lacking the ability to bear children, men have come to overvalue the part they play by worshipping their own genitals. As their sexual activity is the only active part they play in child-bearing, the extent of their involvement needs to be exaggerated in their own eyes. Men are seen to be different from women in the way they regard sex, often being accused of attaching too little importance to the emotional aspects of lovemaking. Perhaps if they had the potential to become pregnant and to carry a child for nine months, their attitude to sex might become more than recreational, the link between the act of coitus and children less tenuous, their genitals less central and their sexuality more diffused throughout their bodies. But as it is, phallic worship goes back to our earliest history and seems to embrace most cultures as a common symbol of power and potency.

Man's fear of castration dominates his behaviour; he dreads the prospect of being emotionally, physically, sexually or intellectually overpowered. This is a contest he must not lose. Because his world is peopled by winners and losers and little mercy is extended to the vanquished, he finds great difficulty in believing in equality. Therefore he will fight for his symbolic manhood even when no contest exists. Men are dangerous but women are the ultimate castrators, able to invoke the sorcery that emasculates men. Woman's profound connectedness with life and the future affords her great latent power, and it is this power that men both fear and desire. Woman's ability to sever man's tenuous link with her procreative power is the stuff of male nightmares.

When I was a teenager, I remember the stories that would circulate among boys about women who had teeth in their vaginas, and of people who after sexual intercourse were unable to separate, the man's penis being permanently trapped in the woman's vagina. This fear of the *vagina dentata* goes very deep in men.

Men have to act, do, in order to feel useful, and it is through his doing that they gain purpose and value. Through doing, men are connected. Common activities such as sport or work give them a semblance of intimacy and a temporary sense of cohesion.

Man the hero has been very much part of our culture and of other cultures. But the problem with heroism is that deeds of strength and courage are not needed every day. Great deeds are no longer helpful markers of a person's fitness to inspire; it is the commonplace events that give direction to our lives. (Just look at St George and the Dragon: up comes George on a white charger, shining armour, lance at the ready. He slays the dragon at great personal cost and rescues the maiden. What happens then? The maiden mightn't be too happy about all this: 'What do you think you are doing, galloping round the countryside in that ridiculous outfit? I was just getting him to eat out of my hand when you came along and killed him . . .' And even if she is grateful for being rescued, how will she feel if St George takes up maiden-rescuing for a living? She won't feel too happy about all those other grateful maidens hanging around, will she?)

We need only think about the tragic spectacle of men who were trained to fight for their country, wandering the streets after the war was over, or sitting at home, lost and discarded, being, in the words of Eric Bogle, 'forgotten heroes of forgotten wars'. Men are left with models of maleness that don't in any way reflect or depict a lifestyle. And the picture is no more optimistic if one considers national folk heroes, such as Ned Kelly. He, in fact, exemplifies all those aspects of maleness that men need to abandon. A man of his time, he was arrogant, fearless, courageous and anti-authority and he stayed defiant to the last. Perhaps the time has come to bury Ned for good and to strip his deeds of the romanticism that time allows, to look for more suitable models of maleness.

When society no longer needs hunters and warriors, these roles need to be redirected to some purpose that is self-sustaining. Work for work's sake, the accumulation of wealth and possessions are inadequate ways of achieving a sense of worth, love or intimacy. In fact, they are the antithesis of those needs. Men will only be able to find themselves by turning their backs on role models that lead to supremacy and isolation. Their lives will need to include women and children and other men, not peripherally but centrally.

The challenge for men is to avoid their natural reaction to threat and to reach out to other people, rather than out to things or tasks. New Age men, with their self-preoccupation and tendency to look for connectedness in the rarefied atmosphere of men's groups, appear self-indulgent and irrelevant to most men's lives. We need to start somewhere, and I can't help feeling that through political and social action the greatest changes can be made to the institutionalised moulds that dictate men's lives. Work, material goods, education and parenting all need to be re-examined in the light of new goals for men. We must begin to address the problems in those major areas of our society that entrench and reinforce characteristics that alienate men from themselves and from each other.

We are being asked to become the so-called 'Clever Country', to stop being suppliers of primary produce and raw materials and to learn to sell our brain power instead of our muscle. But having national goals is pointless if they do not include statements about quality of life. It is very easy for politicians to mouth platitudes about childcare, education and poverty, and even to try and address these issues through social welfare policy. However, close examination reveals that we have no policies that address the problems of the family in a comprehensive way. Taxation, education, health, social services, employment, environment, defence and all the other indivdual government departments impact on the functioning of the family to a greater or lesser extent. Yet, too often the policies of the individual departments contradict the efforts of other departments to address particular issues.

Just as we needed an Office for the Status of Women to examine the effects of particular legislation on women and their aspirations, just as we now expect all proposals for new development to be subjected to an environmental impact statement before being enacted, so we need to develop a national policy on the family. Present and future legislation could then be coordinated to direct our decision-making and social policy towards quality of life issues for ourselves and our children. As long as the critical issues of lifestyle and quality are left to economists to determine, economic rationalism will be the likely outcome. Imagine the fuss if we read headlines like 'National treasures worth $100 billion left to decay, declared worthless'. Our unwillingness to take seriously the need to re-examine our priorities in relation to the family and its support does just that. Children are being neglected through short-sighted policies that place more emphasis on defence than on education and employment.

The workplace has to change, and not just in terms of work practices. Changes such as enterprise bargaining address only the economics of employment, not the social aspects. If men are to be drawn back into a more central role in the family, industry must play a part. Working hours need to be more flexible to accommodate the needs of parenting. Part-time work, job sharing, flexitime, paternity leave, leave without pay, retraining following long periods of child rearing — all these things will make it easier for men to be with their families. But these changes are not enough: hearts and minds need to change. Until the ethos of mangement changes, nothing will be achieved. The very nature of business is competition, and consequently those who rise to the top of an organisation are those who have been most successfully competitive.

But this means that we tend to have organisations led by people, both men and women, who have placed their own careers above all else. And a look at the family life of our leaders of commerce and industry reveals a sorry picture, with wives and children coming a poor last in terms of time priorities. They do well financially, but certainly not in emotional terms. And how can we expect a man whose whole life is his work, to look kindly on his junior staff when they ask for time off to pick up the children from school or when they are sick?

Employers can only start to tackle the problem of an employee who is torn by conflicting demands — wife and children versus career — if it is seen to benefit the company in the long run. The old notion that it is possible to dump problems at the door of the office and then act as if they did not exist is a classic male attitude, the same mechanistic model that got men into so much trouble in the past. It is surely obvious that telling a parent who is worried about a sick child to forget about it achieves nothing except frustration. Work performances will inevitably be affected, because we are not robots, no matter how much we try to be. If employers want maximum performance from employees, they must accept the totality of their lives and incorporate that reality into corporate policy. The organisations that have already taken this step are reaping the rewards of reduced staff turnover, improved productivity and improved staff and management relations. These changes can take place, even without the necessity to address the wider social issues. This is just good management practice.

And a father's preoccupation with his role as breadwinner is no longer acceptable in the twentieth and twenty-first centuries; continuing to be obsessed by this need to provide the material comforts for the family, robs all the family — and consequently society — of a man's unique contribution. If men's sperm gives them a slender hold on the development of the embryo, they can still be substantially involved with the children, and through this connection have emotional links with the next generation. By becoming involved with the rearing of their children, men can reawaken the child inside them, the part of them with the capacity to be emotional, soft, afraid, spontaneous, creative, joyful.

In order for men to move back into their families, however, women will have to tolerate their presence. For a long time the primary caregiving role has been the almost exclusive province of women, and has been their major source of power and influence in a world dominated by men. Women will probably find, as men have done, that there is a big difference between rhetoric and reality when it comes to sharing power. Often the exclusion of fathers is quite subtle because a woman's unconscious motivation stops her from questioning her expectation that she is the most suitable nurturing parent. The fact that most of us were brought up in homes in which the nurturing of the children was the almost exclusive province of our mothers, makes it hard for us to believe that it was not always so and that this is not the only way for families to operate. The tendency to repeat patterns of parenting is very strong in us all, even to the extent that we will repeat those parental behaviours that we vowed to exclude from our own parenting. Women will expect to be principal nurturers; men will stand aside and let them. This sense of inevitability in parenting roles can lead to silly divisions that defy reason.

Some men would clearly fulfil the role of primary nurturer better than their partner, yet this is rarely acknowledged and acted upon.

Men and women will continue to tread different paths that diverge rather than converge. The women's movement has certainly liberated women — but for what? If their liberation leads them to take the places that men have previously occupied, then big deal. We men have been there, and it's no victory. Men need women, and vice versa. Without each other, we have nothing. So let us ignore the strident voices on both sides of the gender debate who mistakenly believe that men and women must fight. Our children deserve a better deal than that.

Men are stuck in roles with expectations that prevent them, despite their longing to do so, from showing anything other than their heroic, competitive, tough exteriors. They feel that masculinity is based on power, control, sexuality, achievement and responsibility — all of which inhibit their true capacity for self-expression and love, and their need for intimacy. Like the Tin Man in *The Wizard of Oz*, men long for the ability to show their hearts, their soft centres. But the Tin Man didn't have to travel to Oz to find a heart: he discovered he had had one all along. He just didn't believe in himself enough to show it, and had to find the environment in which it could be revealed.

Mateship has served men well in the past. It is a relationship that by its very nature allows men to endure and survive in times of hardship and to join together in celebration. Its major flaw lies in its inability to easily adapt to the changing needs of men. In a society less beset by hardship, the need for men to stand together as mates is less important than the need to relate to women and children. Role models need to be re-examined and changed, and flexibility needs to be introduced so that friendship is valued more than mateship. Friendship is devoid of the rigid codes of behaviour that characterise mateship, as it includes vulnerability, non-competitive association and intimacy without the need for an external threat.

The time has come to value mateship for its contribution to our survival and development but to replace it with friendship. For it is only through friendship that men can grow, and realise their potential for true intimacy and love.

As long as men can hide from themselves and each other behind the masks of competition and mateship, their lives will remain truncated — and men will continue to be denied access to a half of themselves that can enrich their lives. The challenge is there. Some men have taken the plunge, the rest of us have yet to follow — not out of a feeling of despair but out of a desire for growth and fulfilment.

Useful Organisations

For those people who wish to explore further any of the issues contained in this book, I have compiled a brief list of possible contacts or starting points. As the men's movement is still in its infancy, this data may rapidly become out of date. I therefore suggest the following organisations and individuals as access points to the Australian network. (See the telephone book for your state details.)

• Marriage counselling agencies • Area health centres • Centacare • Family Life • Family Planning Association • Gay Line • Marriage Guidance • Unifam

New South Wales:
Men's Development Centre, Allan Tegg (02) 555 8753
Sydney Men's Network, Paul Whyte (02) 550 40533

Victoria:
Men International, Robert Ware (03) 449 5906

South Australia:
C.A.M.H.S. Child Adolescent Mental Health Services
Dulwich Centre, Carrington Street, Adelaide (08) 223 3966
Bower Place, Glen Osmond Road, Eastwood (08) 373 1299

Tasmania:
Richard Bryden (003) 95 1365
Adult Education Hobart (002) 30 7325
(for courses 'Understanding the Men's Movement' and 'Listening to Robert Bly')

Reading List

Amato, P., *Children in Australian Families: the Growth of Competence*, Prentice Hall, Sydney, 1987. (Provides further reading to Dr. Don Edgar's details.)

Barz, Helmut, *For Men, Too: A Greatful Critique of Feminism*, Chiron Publications, Illinois, 1991.

Bly, Robert, *Iron John: A Book About Men*, Element Books, England, 1991.

Byrski, Liz, *Under the Influence: Growing Up in Alcoholic Families*, Collins Dove, Melbourne, 1987.

Colman, Arthur & Libby, *The Father: Mythology and Changing Roles*, Chiron Publications, Illinois, 1988.

David, Deborah S. & Brannon, Robert (eds), *The Forty-Nine Percent Majority: The Male Sex Role*, Addison Publishing Co., New York, 1976.

Farrell, Warren, *The Liberated Man: Beyond Masculinity,* Random House, New York, 1974.

Flannagan, Jack & Carol, *Working Parents: Happy Families*, Angus & Robertson, Sydney, 1987.

Keen, Sam, *Fire in the Belly: On Being a Man*, Bantam Books, New York, 1992.

Metcalf, A. & Humpheries, M. (eds), *The Sexuality of Men*, Pluto, London, 1985.

Rolls, Eric, *Celebration of the Senses*, Penguin Books, Melbourne, 1984.

Russell, Graeme, *A Practical Guide for Fathers*, Thomas Nelson, Melbourne, 1983.

— *The Changing Role of Fathers*, UQP, St. Lucia, 1983.

Bibliography

Bean, Charles, *The Official History of Australia in the War of 1914-1918*, vol. 1, *The Story of Anzac*, Angus & Robertson, Sydney, 1921.

Bonney, Roseanne, *Interim Report No. 1*, Bureau of Crime Statistics and Research, 26 Sept. 1985, p. 28.

Corris, Peter, quote taken from *Yacker 3: Australian Writers Talk About Their Work*, Candida Baker, Pan Books, Sydney, 1989, p. 59.

Dixson, Miriam Joyce, *The Real Matilda*, Penguin Books, Melbourne, 1983, p. 81.

Edgar, Don, 'The Role of the Father', The Australian Institute of Family Studies, Melbourne, 1990.

Faust, Beatrice, *Women, Sex and Pornography*, Penguin Books, Melbourne, 1980, p. 2.

Horne, Donald, *The Lucky Country: Australia Today*, Penguin Books, Baltimore, 1965, p. 64.

Hughes, Robert, *The Fatal Shore*, Pan Books, London, 1987, p. 264.

Manning, Frederic, *The Middle Parts of Fortune*, St. Martins Press, New York, 1977, ch. 7.

Pasick, P. S., *The Family Therapy Networker*, Family Therapy Network Press, May/June 1990, U.S.A.

Pittman, Frank, 'The Masculine Mystique', *The Family Therapy Networker*, Family Therapy Network Press, May/June 1990, U.S.A.

Porter, Hal, 'On the Ridge', *Selected Stories*, Angus & Robertson, Sydney, 1971, p. 77.

Stead, Christina, *Letty Fox: Her Luck*, Angus & Robertson, Sydney, 1974, ch. 27.

Summers, Anne, *Damned Whores and God's Police: The Colonisation of Women in Australia*, Penguin Books, Melbourne, 1975, p. 462, 32.

Townsend, Helen, *Baby Boomers: Growing Up in Australia in the 1940s, 50s and 60s*, Simon & Schuster Australia, Sydney, 1988, p. 7.

INDEX